STE

COLLE...

The front cover shows a part of the East Town of Crediton as drawn by John Norden in 1598. The map is part of the Terrier which Norden collated for the information of William Killigrew who acquired the manor of Crediton in 1595.

The original map was destroyed in a fire at Creedy Park in 1915; fortunately a copy of it had been made in the 19th. century which was presented to the Governors of the Church by Arthur Onslow Sillifant of Combe House, himself a Governor. That copy is now in the Devon Record Office in Exeter.

The reproduction from which our cover was taken has been drawn, photographed and inscribed by R.E. Langhorne, A.E. Labbett, Muriel Grimes and Caroline Grant.

The Stephenson Collection

Generously supported by:

Queen Elizabeth Community College

Villages in Action
Rural Creative Project Fund

Greystones Publishing
Greystones House
Park Road
Crediton
Devon EX17 3ES

INTRODUCTION

Since I started teaching creative writing in 1988 I must have worked with 150 writers. What I have found so exciting is the level of talent that lies hidden behind the front doors of Devon.

Everyone is so different - the young mothers seeking the mental stimulation their daily routine lacks, the elderly looking for ways to reflect on their lives, and the middle-aged who feel they'd like to be a writer when they grow up.

The styles are also so different. When I give a group of ten people a subject to write about, the diversity of treatment is stunning. "Obsession" conjured up a woman who makes herself into a transistor radio for Richard Kemp, for Richard Gard it conjured up a very different picture.

Yet one thing that all these writers who come to my classes share, is a lack of belief in their future as a writer.

It's a lonely world for that breed rather dismissively referred to as "the unknown writer". I sometimes wonder whether there shouldn't be a tomb, at the British Library perhaps, where published writers could lay a wreath in relief that they are not lying there beneath the stone slab. How many Shakespeares, Tolstoys and Austens have been buried, their work unread, their genius untapped because they didn't believe in their talent or didn't know what to do with it?

My task as a teacher of creative writing is similar to that of a parent - to help my charges identify their skills and then develop the confidence to present them to the appropriate outlet in the appropriate manner.

I make no apologies for boasting that many of those writers in my groups have gone on to be published. Some, like Sylvia Baker, have won awards. They have done so not because of me, all

I did was to help them recognise the talent that lay within their work and say "Go for it !"

Writers are people wishing to communicate, but without the means to get their work published, their experiences, stories and feelings fall on deaf ears. The resulting sense of isolation can be crushing, which is why I am so very grateful to Queen Elizabeth Community College the Villages in Action Rural Creative Projects Fund and Mid Devon District Council for making this book possible.

Mary Stephenson

The illustrations are by local artists and photographers. Grateful thanks to
Barbara Aldridge
Marjorie St. John
June Lukins
Elizabeth Brown
Roy Knowles
Richard Kemp

Barbara Aldridge

Foreword

I am delighted to be writing this foreword to the Crediton Writers' Class anthology and to have the chance to give a little encouragement to those whose stories appear in its pages. Inspiration is undoubtedly the basic ingredient of creativity and there is nothing quite as uplifting as seeing one's work in print. And reading your work in book form can be useful in enabling you to see it in a detached way, as others see it, an almost impossible thing to do when it is on your own sheet of paper, on your own desk.

People write for many different reasons. Often we begin because we find it pleasurable, fulfilling. But, as I expect many of the writers within these pages have discovered, once started it's hard to stop. The desire for recognition and praise enters the equation, publication becomes the goal. I say goal instead of dream because that's how you should treat it, something you are working towards not something you just dream about. Don't let anyone tell you it's impossible for new writers to get published these days. A few years ago I was in the same position as you, learning and hoping, now I work full time as a writer and have two books in the shops. It happened for me it can happen for you. Don't ever give up!

I wish you all every success,

Sylvia Baker

Chapter One

A Sense of Place

The Yeoford Explosion	**David Browning**
Glorious Past, Uncertain Future?	**Richard the Miller**
On Ghosts & Legends	**June Lukins**
A Local Building	**Val Williams**
The Beast or Exmoor	**Val Williams**
Lambing Time	**June Lukins**
Reeve Castle	**Val Williams**
Ernest Bevin - The Country Boy	**Jeff Kingaby**
Wild Exe	**June Lukins**

THE YEOFORD EXPLOSION

by

DAVID BROWNING

In the run up to D-day 1944, one of the many logistical problems that General Eisenhower's HQ Staff had to solve, was where to stockpile the vast quantity of munitions required for the assault on the Normandy beaches. The places chosen had to be secure from the searching eyes of the Luftwaffe for two main reasons. Firstly, the allied plan was to actively mislead the Germans into thinking that the main axis of assault for the invasion of France would be through Dover, across the Pas de Calais, at the channel's narrowest point. An obvious build up of forces around West Country ports would have alerted them to the fact that the actual target was Normandy. Secondly, if the Germans had detected any new munitions dumps either by aerial reconnaissance or spying activity, they would certainly have attempted to destroy them by aerial bombardment. If this had been successful the allies would have been forced to postpone the invasion for at least a year. It was therefore decided not to concentrate the war materials at fixed locations but to keep them aboard freight trucks in various railway sidings where any build up would not be so obvious. One of the railway sidings used was at Yeoford which had a shunting yard capable of handling well over a hundred standard goods wagons and it is estimated that in the week before D-day the equivalent of four thousand tons of TNT was parked right in the middle of Yeoford village. Had the enemy discovered the whereabouts of these explosives and attacked them, the whole of Yeoford would have been destroyed, along with much of the surrounding area.

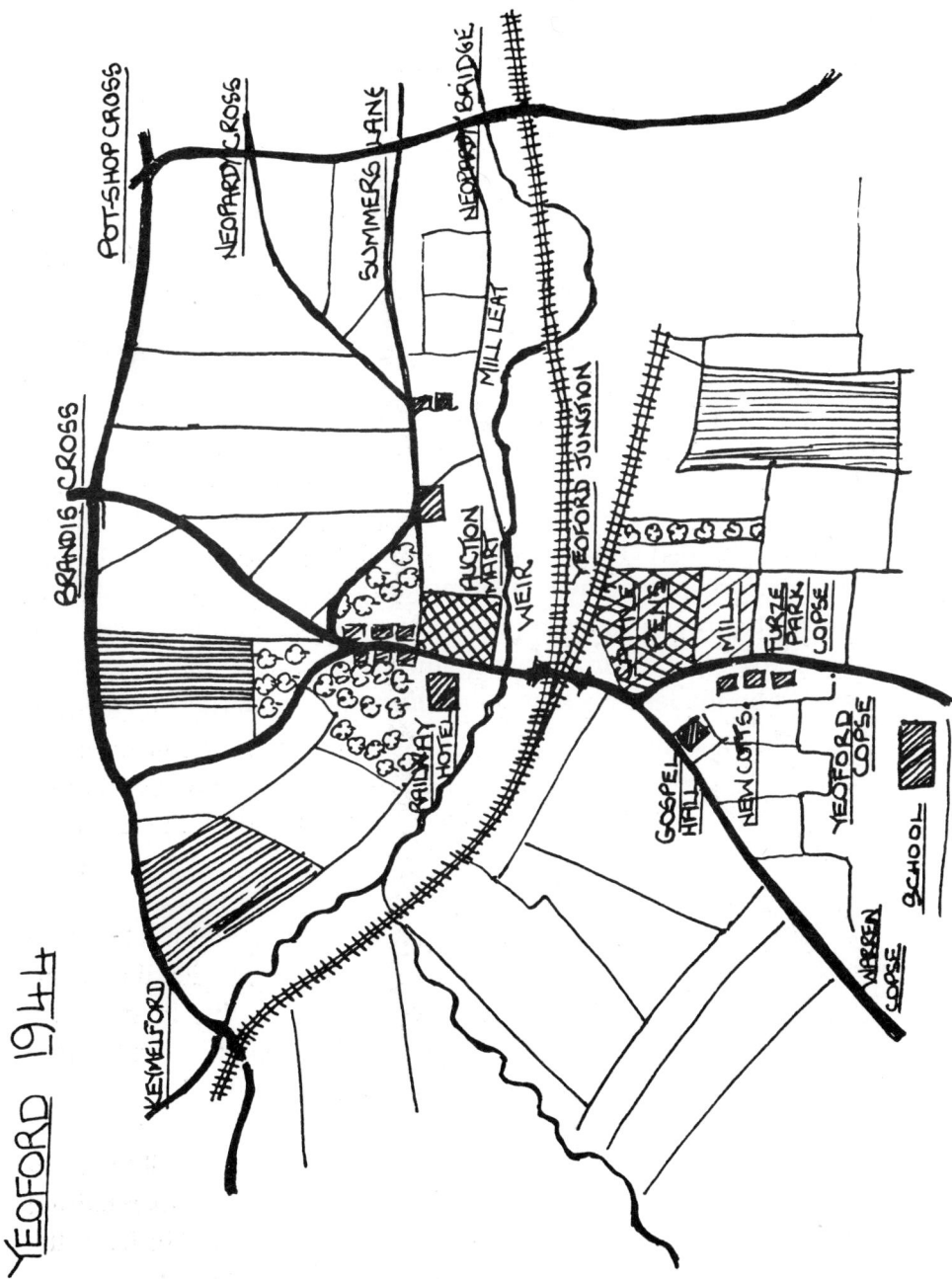

Since the war, with the building of three estates and several individual homes, Yeoford's population has multiplied several times but the original layout is still easily visible. The railway sidings have been removed, as have the waiting rooms on one platform and the passenger bridge across the lines, but the road and river bridges are still in use. Station Road is much the same as it always was. There's a large cob house, with walls of sub-soil and straw, and several brick cottages on one side, and the pub, originally called Ware's Station Hotel, later renamed the Mare and Foal, next to a double thatched cottage on the other. As the road to Crediton climbs out of the village on the left is a 16th century farm house, together with its labourers cottages, and on the right another substantial cob house. Here the road divides to give an alternative route to Crediton and about two hundred yards outside the village it passes yet another cob farmhouse. In the other direction the road crosses two bridges and divides at a T-junction. The left fork passes over a hump backed bridge by the village store with a row of farm cottages and the school on the right. The site of the old timber company, the largest local employer until 1983, is on the left. It's now a housing estate. The right fork at the T-junction goes towards Hittisleigh village. This road goes uphill gradually for about two miles and a pair of brick cottages and two ancient cob farm houses are clearly visible from the edge of Yeoford.

What would have happened, if, on a fateful day one week before D-day, a lone Messerschmitt had flown in low under the radar, penetrated the Exe estuary, followed the railway line inland from St.David's and dropped a single cluster of incendiary bombs onto four thousand tons of TNT parked at Yeoford Station ?

A few seconds after impact a great fireball, visible from Dartmoor, would have engulfed the whole station and marshalling yard, and a destructive shockwave would have raced out from the epicentre at a speed of over seven hundred miles an hour, destroying all in its path. As it raced down Station Road - pub, cottages, farmhouses - all would have either been flattened by the blast or set on fire, or both. Some of the force would then have been dissipated as it went over the crest of the hill above the village, but some would have been reflected and hurtled back westward a fraction of a second after the main blast. The double shockwave would have immediately engulfed the store, destroyed the cottages and set the timber yard on fire. The stone construction of the school may well have saved it from entire obliteration, but it also would have been very severely damaged. In the open farmland along the Hittisleigh Road the hedges would have caught fire and the farmhouses and cottages would have been severely damaged or destroyed. At about two miles from the station the upward slope of the land would have diverted the destructive force of the shock waves and dissipated them skywards. The fire brigade would have raced from Crediton and Okehampton, put out the many fires still burning on their arrival and helped any lucky survivors. They would have wondered at the vast scene of devastation, second only to the grim scene at Exeter after the Biedekker raid the year before. For months afterwards people would have travelled for miles to view the crater that had been Yeoford Station and the ruins that had been Yeoford Village.

But it didn't happen - Yeoford never featured as a Luftwaffe target and soon after June 6th 1944 the explosives followed the troops to France and the danger was over.

Glorious Past, Uncertain Future ?

by

RICHARD THE MILLER

For thirty-two generations this building has earned its keep. Why is it my generation, growing up in the '50s and '60s who takes away the source of power and cannot find a role for a working historic building? What is it about my generation that makes it so ready to neglect and lay waste? Perhaps it has something to do with the National Dried Milk and orange juice available in the 1940s and '50s.

Just missing inclusion in the Doomsday book, Stockleigh Mill started work around the year 1200, as the estate water mill for the village of Stockleigh Pomeroy. In 1293 the mill prospered and was worth four shillings per year under the management of 'Richard the Miller'. All the tenants of the manor were compelled to grind their corn there and in 1305 the mill was worth ten shillings. Just over a century later Stockleigh Mill was a fulling mill for the expanding wool industry in the Middle Ages, where the cloth was cleaned, shrunk and thickened in water. Twenty years later arable land had dropped to a farthing an acre and had become rough pasture. Meadow land fell from two shillings to sixpence and the mill was worth one shilling and eightpence per annum. The Black Death had arrived in Devon.

Bubonic Plague hit Dorset in 1348 and within weeks towns and villages in Devon recorded the effects. For three hundred years the disease lived on, spread by the huge population of flea-infested rats. During this time the mill faltered but continued to function as trade allowed. Fortunes rose in Mid Devon during the 1600s with great movement of people through Plymouth and Exeter and rural areas prospered providing food. The mill reverted to a corn mill and the miller's cottage was built at the end of the century. Eleven people were known to live at Stockleigh Mill, but it is hard to imagine where they all slept.

Work continued daily until 1938 when a storm damaged the weir serving the mill leat. The leat was never repaired and, until 1954, the mill operated only when sufficient head of water was available. At that time the mill was purchased by the sitting tenant who sold everything of value, including the wooden mill wheel, and left two years later. He had seen his livelihood disappear and reclaimed whatever he could.

The final indignity came in the early '70s when the council widened the road, filled in the mill leat and left this proud building literally high and dry. So what becomes of an 800 year old, large garden shed with a unique high roof? It is said that cob buildings should have a good hat and slippers, so, in 1991, the mill was rethatched. It now stands waiting.

Waiting for a reason why its ageing timbers should be repaired. Waiting for its time to come again. Waiting for a reason to thrive. Not, please, as a modernised Wimpey house. It has never been occupied and never had glass in its windows. No Peach Melba bathroom suite should be fitted here.

Not to survive as a relic but a functional working asset. Earning its keep. Supporting the parish. Surviving the generations. Will the Rural White Paper really allow more relaxed planning and the development of business in traditional buildings, rather than soulless industrial units? Maybe.

Stockleigh Mill is patient. Stockleigh Mill is waiting.

On Ghosts & Legends

by

JUNE LUKINS

Our busy lambing time over for another season, I turned my attention to Dartmoor and my search for public houses with interesting tales attached to them.

My first is a rather sad one and involves a child crying piteously and continuously in an upstairs room, at the old Inn at Widecombe in the Moor, sometimes for hours at a time. When the door is opened the crying stops immediately and of course there is nobody there. Which is not altogether unlike the story surrounding the Nobody Inn at Doddiscombeleigh. It was converted from what was a terrace of early 16th century cottages and older stables, once occupied by some of the miners who worked locally. The tale involves a landlord of some fifty years ago, who died in Exeter Hospital. His funeral was held but an empty coffin was buried. The bearers thought it was rather light but no-one liked to mention it as the poor man had been very ill for a considerable time. Then a retired policeman on holiday from Norfolk in the seventies, visited the pub and confirmed the story. He had been a probationary constable at the coroner's office at the time and remembered that an exhumation order had been granted to allow the grave to be opened up, which begs the question,
"If there was nobody in, then what happened to the body ?"

Fortunately there was no such mystery with the wonderful tale about the 14th century tinners pub called the New House or New Inn (to differentiate it from the Old Inn of the same period at Widecombe). It stood on the opposite side of the road to the present Warren House Inn, on the moor near Postbridge. A traveller arrived on a bleak mid-winters night, after the moor had been snowbound for several weeks, and was accommodated in a room containing a large chest. His curiosity getting the better of him, he lifted the lid and peered in, to find that it contained the corpse of a man with skin of unusual whiteness. In a state of shock he ran down to the bar - thinking he had uncovered a murder victim, to be told by the landlord,

"There's nothing to worry about, 'tis only feyther. He died three weeks ago, but the weather's been too bad to get 'un to Tavistock for burial, so mother salted 'un down so's he'd keep better. She's a dab hand at saltin'down is mother."

That inn was burnt down and replaced by Warren House in 1845 and some say that a shovelful of still hot embers from the remains of the old pub were carried across the road and used to start a fire in the new hearth, where it has burned continuously ever since.

Another interesting hearth is to be found at the Oxenham Arms at South Zeal, which has a huge granite slab over it. It also has a legend....

The hotel, situated almost at the foot of Cosdon Hill, was reputedly built by the monks in the 11th century and first licensed in 1477. It is named after the Oxenhams whose history dates back to Elizabeth I, and whose family home is Oxenham Manor, which stands about a mile from South Zeal and is said to be linked to the hotel by a tunnel, starting from a well in the garden.

The family were haunted by a white breasted bird and its presence in the vicinity of a family member shortly preceded that person's death. Although it must be said that some were already close to death when the bird appeared! A particularly tragic incident involved a Lady Margaret whose father saw it fluttering nearby on the day before her wedding, but said nothing as he did not want to distress her. As she stood at the altar a jealous ex-lover rushed into the church, stabbed her in the back, then pulled out the knife and stabbed himself with it also.

Another Oxenham, on feeling a little poorly, sighted the bird, sat up in bed and proclaimed :

"I may be sick, but I'm not that sick." - only to die a few days later.

Whilst on the subject of birds, the Plume of Feathers at Princetown has a rather indiscreet ghost. Inhabiting the original ladies loo on the east side of the building, it frightens it's temporary occupants so much that ladies run out of there with their knickers down around their knees! It follows some to the bedrooms too and forces them to hang on tightly to their bedsheets as it tries to tweak them off in the middle of the night. Perhaps it is looking for the letterbox rumoured to be hidden at this inn ?

Also at Princetown and standing a little way from the Plume, is another public house. Though not in the same sense as the others, a public house nonetheless; grey, desolate and guaranteed to strike chill into the hearts of all those who stay there. This tale is about a prisoner called David Davis who was sent to Dartmoor Prison in 1879 and over two terms of imprisonment served a total of fifty years until he died there in 1929. For a large part of his stay he was trusted to work as a shepherd on the moor. He enjoyed the work so much that at the end of his first term he asked to be employed in the same capacity on a permanent basis. This request was refused, so he immediately re-offended and was sent back to prison and "his" flock. So dedicated was he, that since his death a ghostly shepherd has been seen briefly from time to time as he moves among the sheep, safeguarding them at night during the lambing season.

A LOCAL BUILDING

by

VAL WILLIAMS

Sprawling at the end of Crediton main street is the Parish Church or to give it its full title :

**The Collegiate Church of the Holy Cross
& the Mother of Him who Hung Thereon.**

It can look warm and inviting with the sun shining on its red sandstone walls and glinting on the two rows of plain glass windows. The square bell tower with its four symmetric pinnacles sits firmly in the centre of the building.

A Saxon cathedral, probably of wooden construction, was dedicated on the site in 933. The actual stone building began much later with work continuing slowly throughout the 13th and 14th centuries. At the beginning of the 15th century the nave was found to be in such a poor state that it could not be used as a parish church. Therefore rebuilding began in 1410 and continued at intervals until modern times.

After the dissolution of the religious communities by Henry V111, which included the Collegiate Church of Crediton in 1536, the King's Commissioners removed from the canons all their rights to the church and its lands. The town people raised £300 and this was paid to the King. In consideration of this payment Edward V1 granted a charter to the church in 1547 incorporating 12 governors who would not take up their full duties until the death of the then Rector of Exminster. No one knows why this proviso was applied - but the rector lived to a great old age and it wasn't until

1580, during the reign of Elizabeth 1, that the first vicar was appointed.

Walking carefully up the cobbled path to the present church one notices the old gravestones, some set at odd angles with grass long at their feet. Stepping down into the porch and pushing hard on the heavy oak door one enters the church itself and is immediately impressed by its size. The nave stretches for 72 feet with a high carved roof overhead. The arched pillars, standing in two rows, head towards the alter with two crosswise arches separating the choirstalls from the congregation and supporting the central tower.

Above the first tower arch is the overpowering memorial to General Sir Redvers Buller of Boer War fame. It is an enormous piece of work consisting of a frieze of Victoria crosses above which are 15 panels containing armorial bearings, warrior saints and mosaic panels all flanking the big central cross. Above this is a stone representation of Christ with martial saints on either side. The lower half of the tower is the earliest part of the present building, the piers of which are about 1150, decorated in typical Norman fashion with zigzags, snakes and birds.

Behind the altar one can enter through a pair of screens into the Lady Chapel, losing immediately the warmth and airiness of the main building, and exchanging it for the cold and mustiness that is associated with old places. Two stained glass windows depicting events in the life of Our Lady filter the light and cast shadows, adding to the general gloom.

Wandering back into the main body of the church via the south choir aisle, one finds the entry to the vestry with Museum and Governors' Rooms over. These rooms form a separate unit and are known as the Chapter House. There are two oak angels in the church still with their medieval paint - the story goes that there were originally 12 angels but ten were burnt by the governors to keep themselves warm in the corporation chamber. Today, even with modern heating installed, the church can still-be very cold at times, so perhaps one should have a little sympathy for them.

South West Door

The pulpit is unusually made of stone with carved statuettes of the four evangelists encircling it. Opposite stands the wooden eagle lectern evidently carved from a live model in 1894. The pews are of the open bench variety - the old box ones having been removed in 1887. Just inside the south door stands a square Norman font, reputedly the oldest item to be seen. Its plainness is relieved by an elaborately carved 20th century wooden cover which is winched up above when a baptism takes place. A rather worrying procedure for mothers one would imagine.

There have been some notable vicars in the church history. John Rudall (1790-1835) wrote to the Governors in early 1800 asking them to forward his stipend as his chest was bad and he had to live by the sea. In 1805 he was found to be serving as a Naval Chaplain at the Battle of Trafalgar and presumably drawing two salaries. Another was Samuel Rowe (1835-53), apparently a keen horseman he spent a lot of his time riding on Dartmoor and eventually wrote a monumental book called "Perambulations on Dartmoor". Thirdly, Charles Felton Smith (1853-1900) was chosen vicar by default. The favourite, a Mr.Eardley, was given to long sermons of the "fire & brimstone" variety. One particularly fierce one gave offence to so many of the Governors that Mr Smith was appointed instead.

There are regular services held on Sundays and some weekdays. One recent service was to include pets. Children from the area duly presented them to the vicar standing in front of the church. "Smallest first," he instructed, and so they came - a grasshopper, gerbils, hamsters, rabbits, cats and after a suitablepause, dogs. After a short prayer when they all behaved impeccably, they returned to their seats with their young owners. Everything went well until the congregation began the first hymn, as they raised their voices so the dogs raised theirs ! There were barks, whines, wails and moans. Everyone was convulsed with laughter and found it very difficult to continue. The offending dogs and their owners, were asked very kindly to leave, and the service was resumed without further interruptions.

Last year an episode of "Songs of Praise" was recorded at the Parish Church. It necessitated lots of equipment - mobile vans outside, cables lying around everywhere and even scaffolding inside the church to enable the electricians to fix additional lighting. While aloft they kindly fitted new bulbs to the present system. The church was beautifully decorated for Candlemas - lovely swathes of ivy encircled the pillars and candles in silver holders (previously lent by members of the congregation) clustered amongst them. The recording took much longer than anyone had imagined - there were two hours of rehearsals followed by 3 hours of TV audio recording the first evening, and another 2 hours of rehearsal and 3 1/2 hours for the video recording the next night. It really was a survival of the fittest - stopping, starting, waiting to see if it was OK and then beginning all over again. It was also very wearing to follow instructions by looking at the conductor all the time, never at the cameras which were propelled up and down the aisles.

It had been quite an evening and everyone was parched by the close. There was some disappointment a few weeks later, when the programme was shown on the TV. There were a lot of outside shots, but those of the actual service, seemed so short they didn't truly reflect all the work put into it. There is a feeling of peace and tranquillity in the church for all who wish to enjoy it. A place of prayer that has continued over the centuries.

THE BEAST OF EXMOOR

"The Hound of the Baskervilles ?"

by

VAL WILLIAMS

There has been so much in the news lately about the black puma-like creature stalking the rolling hills of Exmoor, that it's difficult to remember when it all began.

Tales of its existence have abounded for generations, hence Conan Doyle's "Hound of the Baskervilles" was brought into question. According to Ronnie Hoyle (sub-Editor of the Western Morning News) legend changed to fact in 1970 when a farmer's wife and a 14 year old boy from the Tedburn St Mary area, reported seeing a black panther-like animal to the police. A week later a man from Effordsleigh also reported seeing a strange black animal near his home. He watched its progress from his greenhouse, together with two friends. They decided it was "a large black creature, twice the size of a labrador, with a small head and thick hind and fore legs".

Police checked the local zoo at Plymouth and nearby Chipperfield's Circus to see if an animal had gone missing but it had not. During the next few years there were numerous sightings of the beast in Devon, eventually centering on the wide open space of Exmoor.

The news of its existence became world wide, big game hunters arrived, furnished with shot guns, and even a troop of Royal Marines, but they all failed to catch it dead or alive. It's not just lambs that have been killed, but fully grown rams and ewes, torn or killed with apparent ease. On one farm alone at South Molton, a hundred sheep were devoured over a period of one week. The mass of deer carcasses found near Exeter could not have been the work of poachers and their trained lurcher dogs, as they would have taken home the venison.

As the years have passed so tales of the beast have multiplied, sightings have increased and numerous theories put forward. Popular belief amongst naturalists is that of feral cats, mutants perhaps breeding on Exmoor, evolving over the years to become large enough to kill sheep. A sighting by Trevor Beer (author of The Beast of Exmoor, Fact or Legend?) describes seeing a black panther-type creature at dusk with glowing green eyes. Though always attributed to cats, dogs eyes also glow in the dark.

It has even been suggested that the missing child Genette Tate could have been snatched off her bicycle at Aylesbeare, in August of 1978, by a beast. Her two companions following only a few minutes later found her abandoned bike with the back wheel still spinning. No sound nor sight of a car could explain her sudden disappearance.

Nearer home Barbara Carbonall, who once lived near Bow, spent a lot of time collecting authenticated accounts of the black beast inhabiting the countryside between Copplestone and Torrington. Her findings were reported in a W.I. publication around 1980.

How come **Black Dog** some six miles north of Crediton got its name ? Had someone perhaps, spotted a strange black animal roaming around that area ?

Bringing the tales more up to date, an animal skull found in a river on Bodmin Moor in August '95 was that of a big cat according to Doug Richardson, assistant curator of mammals at London Zoo. The two huge front fangs showed it came from the panther family which includes leopards, jaguars, tigers and lions. After further investigations it was found to have been an elaborate hoax, the skull originating from India, was probably removed from someone's tiger skin rug.

A recent video showing a puma-like creature taken by Wayne Broad at Pawlett, north of Bridgewater, asks the question yet again - Is it the Beast of Exmoor ? Despite petitions to the local MP and the Ministry of Agriculture, no further official investigations are to take place.

The sightings have been so far apart it must be impossible for it to be the same beast. As for the video, could it be a hoax too? What about the photos of the Loch Ness Monster that have never been proved ?

Until the beast is caught, dead or alive, no one can say definitely if it is fact or fiction - legend or myth.

LAMBING TIME

by

JUNE LUKINS

Lambing's almost here again,
my boiler suits are clean.
all piled up on the cupboard
in "sheep dung" shades of green.

I've stuffed the freezer to the brim,
with shepherds' pies and more,
when we crawl back in at half past three
I'll cry - "Here's one I made before".

I've got my hypodermics, and
the vaccine for the lambs.
a 200 pack of elastic bands,
to take care of all the rams.

It's all kept in a bucket
with an orange snap-on lid
My medicinal whisky's in there too,
In the wormer box it's hid.

I look forward to it every year,
It's our farming's annual crop.
But when we've had six weeks of "nights"
I long for them to stop.

REEVE CASTLE

by

VAL WILLIAMS

Reeve Castle lies between the villages of Bow and Zeal Monochorum. It was built at the turn of the century by the eccentric William Carter-Pedler for his bride Lizzie. Approaching it by road it is half hidden by tall trees, the drive is unkempt, tangled bushes obstruct the way adding to the general feeling of mystery and foreboding. Not wanting to intrude on its present owner I determined to find out more about the origins of the castle and its multitalented designer.

William Carter-Pedler was a popular and well respected man, he was a Justice of the Peace and a one time member of Devon County Council. It is reputed that he cycled to work in Exeter, a distance of some eighteen miles. He was a staunch Wesleyan and regularly attended the Bow chapel which he helped to build and played the organ there quite often.

The castle, built in 1900 of cream coloured Barnstaple brick, was of unusual design - to some a Victorian fantasy, to others a Venetian Gothic. Essentially the building is a flat roofed two storey rectangle with projecting turrets to the corners and a three storey entrance porch, above and behind which rises a glass domed observation tower looking like a minaret or large chimney. An extensive iron framed conservatory was built to the left of the main building and the service block to the rear.

Once inside the visitor would have been impressed by the huge organ taking central stage in a massive stairwell with the rooms ranged around it. To the rear was a large billiard room surmounted by a glass dome and the dining and drawing rooms. A galleried staircase led to the first floor rooms. Many of the windows consisted of diamond shaped panes of red, yellow and — blue giving a gentle glow of colour and warmth to the rooms.

Electricity was produced by a number of generators in the outside boiler house, while the castle itself was heated by the numerous underground tunnels lying beneath the floors with heat generated from the boiler. To start the boiler engine one of the servants would have had to cross the bridge connecting the engine house to the top of a tall iron framed tower built nearby. This contained a weight and a pulley connected to the boiler engine. When the weight was dropped the engine started.

The grounds were wonderfully landscaped, there was a Japanese garden including a large concrete lined lake with islands. Paths wound through water gardens, rockeries, flower beds and there were many unusual conifers, about which Mr Carter-Pedler had an expert knowledge. There was also a tennis court and a croquet lawn. With a certain amount of judicious felling of trees extensive views were opened up of the moors.

To this grand house when completed, William, already middle aged, brought his pretty young bride Lizzie. She gave birth to twin girls who sadly died in infancy of scarlet fever. She later had a son who was called Bobby. They were evidently a very happy family and often entertained. There were tennis parties in summer and excursions to Dartmoor, at night there were often games, singing and dancing. Lizzie had an infectious gaiety about her; she was always full of fun and laughter which endeared her to her many friends. Her life changed dramatically when Walter died in 1940 and Bobby left home to work in London. She shut up most of the house and retired to two small rooms at the back. She was not allowed to sell the place because of a proviso in Walter's will. Even after her death in 1956 it was some time before Bobby could dispose of it.

For many years the place lay empty and neglected - plundered and vandalised, stripped of anything of value, until in 1976 the castle and grounds were bought by Harold and Muriel Morley-Sharpe. After seven years of tremendous hard work, sheer determination and a great deal of money, it was restored to its former glory and finally opened as a first class restaurant in '84. Unfortunately it was not a financial success and soon after, the Morley-Sharpes moved out.

Once more the castle lay empty and desolation returned. Not much is known of its present owner and I am sure that is how he wishes it to be.

Ernest Bevin - The Country Boy

by

Jeff Kingaby

As we approach the end of the 20th century, historians will be debating who were the great British politicians and reformers of the century and no doubt among the list will be Lloyd George, Winston Churchill and of course Margaret Thatcher. At the very top should undoubtedly be Ernest Bevin. A man who excelled as an orator and leader of men, founder of the Transport & General Workers Union, Minister of Labour and National Service in Churchill's wartime cabinet and also the post war Foreign Secretary.

Prior to his sudden death in April 1951, he could have claimed some credit for setting up wages councils, The Welfare State, The Marshal Plan (which helped a bankrupt Europe recover after the war) and, possibly his greatest achievement, the founding of NATO which has probably provided us with 50 years of peace; but it is unlikely that he would have voiced his successes. He was a modest man who declined knighthoods and titles on many occasions. The only honour he received was on his death; his ashes were placed in the national shrine - Westminster Abbey.

He disliked fuss. He liked things to be kept simple and practical. No doubt his childhood would have considerably influenced his personality and attitude to life. Whilst most contemporary politicians attended Eton, Harrow, Cambridge or Oxford, Ernest's educational record reads - Winsford, Morchard Bishop, Colbrooke and Hayward's School. At the age of 11 his full time education had finished. His contemporaries became solicitors, barristers and accountants. He became a farm boy on two different farms at Copplestone and later a labourer in Bristol.

Diana Mercy Bevin was 40 years old, on the 7th March 1881, when she gave birth to her sixth son and seventh child, Ernest, at the small village of Winsford, Somerset. Since 1877 she had described herself as a widow, working as a domestic help on farms, in homes and at the Royal Oak Inn. She also acted as the village midwife. She undertook every job she could find to feed her young hungry family. They were described as the poorest in the village. Her only consolation was her burning faith. She was a staunch nonconformist and every Sunday she took her family to the tin chapel in the village and even though Ernest was illegitimate (she refused to name his father) she still treasured her son and treated him no differently from her other six children. When Ernest was eight years old his mother died of a fibrous growth.

It was his half-sister, Mary Pope and her husband George who brought this orphan the thirty miles to Shobrooke Farm in Morchard Bishop, Devon. Although George worked as a railwayman at the Morchard Road Station and probably saw the new standard gauge track introduced on that line in 1892, his family had been tenant farmers since before 1840 at nearby Nathorne Farm. They continued farming at Shobrooke until 1923 when its present owners, Mr & Mrs Shapland bought it.

The villages of North Creedy suffered great poverty and had little contact with the outside world. The poor took care of each other until they could hold on no longer and then left for the big cities. Villagers with spirit became nonconformists to indicate their independence, their rejection of the "Establishment" and their right to be treated equally before God. The school log at Morchard Bishop shows he commenced there on 20th May 1889, three weeks after his mother's death. It had just two classrooms in those days, one for the boys and one for the girls, whereas today it is a thriving five classroomed primary school.

To attend the village school would have necessitated this 8 year old lad walking two miles along footpaths and tracks, now designated as "Two Moors Way", and trodden annually by hundreds of ramblers on their way from Ivybridge to Exmoor. Once called the Mariners Way, it was used by seamen who were laid off on one coast of Devon seeking work on the other coast.

In the following Autumn he moved with his foster parents to a cob and thatched cottage called "Tiddly-Winks", in Copplestone, which is now opposite the mill on the A377. This cottage was seriously damaged by fire a few years ago but has been tastefully restored and rethatched. The current owners have recently opened up the two inglenook fireplaces which would have been used in Ernest's time.

In spite of the poverty of the time, the Popes took good care of their charge for three years but expected him to work hard at home. In Alan Bullock's book "The Life & Times of Ernest Bevin", the local postman describes how he often saw young Ernest in the early hours of the morning getting water from two streams which ran across the hilly fields opposite and cascaded into the ditch adjacent to the main Barnstaple road. Those were the days before pumps were fitted outside houses. Apparently, like so many children of the times, he suffered from terrible chilblains on his hands.

Another chore which was expected of him before leaving for school, was peeling potatoes and cleaning boots. Mark Stevens mentions in his book "Ernest Bevin", that in 1944 when stationed with Winston Churchill in a special train at Droxford, to watch the troops prepare for the invasion of Normandy, Churchill discovered that the Minister of Labour and National Service - as Bevin then was - cleaned his own boots. Horrified that the man responsible for mobilising the entire country had to look after himself, Churchill gave instructions for Bevin to have a batman. Bevin was not keen. "I wouldn't like you to do that, Prime Minister," he said, "I get such splendid ideas when I'm cleaning my boots".
Molotov, the Soviet Foreign Secretary was also horrified when he found Bevin cleaning his own boots.

As there was no school in Copplestone in 1889 he walked the two miles to the old two classroomed school at Colbrooke, which is situated just north of the village and today is just a roofless ruin. Apparently the schoolmaster, Mr Sharland, helped him very considerably with his reading.

Encouraged by his foster parents, Ernest regularly attended the Copplestone "Ebenezer" chapel which had been opened the previous year, and like his mother, remained a staunch nonconformist until he died. The term "Ebenezer" is taken from the Old Testament (1 Samuel 7-12) and means the "Stone of Help" which was very appropriate for that deprived orphan. Today the chapel is the very centre of a thriving village community.

Mrs Pope managed to secure a place in Haywards Boy's School in Crediton and he commenced on 2nd September 1890. Because his brother-in-law worked for the London & South Western Railway Company he managed to obtain a railway pass for Ernest to travel the five miles daily to Crediton. Ernest reached Standard 1V in July 1891 and not only was he entitled to receive a "Labour Certificate", he was also entitled to leave school. However, he remained at that school until 25th March 1892. The exterior of Haywards school has probably changed very little since those days although it is now a primary school.

There is an interesting story that was told some years ago by Dame Georgina Buller, daughter of General Buller. In connection with some charity work she went to see Ernest Bevin whilst he was Minister of Labour but on arrival found his ante room full of people waiting to see him. She had hardly arrived before her name was called and she was ushered into the Minister's office. She was so surprised that she had been invited to jump the queue and asked the Minister why she had received preferential treatment. He replied :

"I wanted to see what you looked like when I heard that you had arrived. As a boy I went to school at Haywards and was caught stealing apples from your father's orchard (at Downes, Crediton) and was given a good hiding."

The Dame congratulated him, adding :

"And look where it got you. You are a Minister."

The interview lasted some time as the great man talked of Crediton.

At the age of eleven years and sixteen days his formal education was completed and he became a farm boy living in at Chaffcombe Farm earning sixpence a week for a ten hour day, six days a week - payable on quarter days. His duties included herding the cows, scaring birds, picking up stones and cutting mangolds and turnips for cattle. In the evening he would read the "Bristol Mercury" newspaper to his employers in front of the fire.

It is not known why he lived in at Chaffcombe Farm and later at Beers Farm on the Okehampton road, because both are within half a mile of "Tiddly-Winks". He commenced his new job in the winter of 1892/3 with Farmer William Snell May, where he managed to double his wages and earn one shilling a week. His career as a farm boy came to an abrupt end in 1894 after a disagreement with Farmer May about the amount of cattle food he had chopped up one morning. Villagers in Copplestone claim that the farmer hid himself in a cupboard to avoid the irate 13 year old who had armed himself with a bill hook. Beer farm is still a working farm today and owned by Farmer May's grandson, Michael.

Ernest's brother Jack had written urging him to join his other five brothers in Bristol and seek his fortune there, so it was not surprising when this 13 year old decided that country life was not for him and joined the hundreds of thousands of poor villagers who had fled to the town since 1870. Taking the train from the tiny Copplestone railway station, he made his way to what was then Britain's second largest city.

WILD EXE

A Poem

by

JUNE LUKINS

Rising in a lonely place and
dancing to a slow dance across the moor.

Butterflies a myriad of tiny winged creatures
buzz and hover, tasting the sweet nectar
of bogbeam and orchid, alighting on wispy cotton grass
then urgently moving on, lives short, no time to waste.

Meandering past quaking bog, holder of dark secrets,
watching, waiting, silently, hungry for the unwary.
Witnessed by buzzards, mewling and wheeling,
catching currents of air & lifted upwards,
to dive, falling and swooping, after movement far below.

Dancing now with a livelier step -
making music of your own.
Twisting and falling over boulders, gathering speed.

Passing ponies with soft eyes and mealy muzzles.
Late born foals sport together, yet alert.
Never too far away from watchful mothers,
lest the sound of rushing water
make them prey to some silent, stalking creature.

You tumble, foaming downwards, to the valley bottom
where deer, who live in the shadow of the woodlands,
forage fitfully, tense, ready to melt silently,
into the shadows of the trees,
at the slightest movement or flash of nostril.

Bursting into the sunshine, shallow banks, scrubby trees,
slowly winding, fish rising, taking flies.
Through fields of grazing sheep and cattle,
who gaze after families on Sundays, children shrieking,
playing with excited pet dogs in the shallows.

Now dark and murky, life struggles to survive
the pollution of human selfishness and indifference.
Between high walls and under noisy highways,
trapped, manipulated, sullen and grey.

Then heading urgently and with relief,
out to the sea's vastness to become "Wild Exe" once more.

CHAPTER TWO

First Love

First Love (1)   **Val Williams**
First Love (2)   **Val Williams**

FIRST LOVE (1)

by

VAL WILLIAMS

My first love was small, red-haired, freckled and 9 years old. He was a lovely boy - kind and helpful - we had great fun together. He was also very serious and declared his love for me and asked me to marry him. He saved his pocket money and eventually bought me a wedding ring. We were duly married over the fence at school with some of his friends as witnesses. Naturally, I couldn't wear the ring at school, so slipped it into my desk to retrieve it before I went home.

Then disaster struck - I couldn't find it. I took all my books out, searched wildly, but it never turned up. I had to confess its loss to my "love" who, rightly, was very annoyed and called the whole thing off immediately. I think his mother had a few words as well.

That was the end of my first love - very short and very sweet. I returned to the village some twenty years later and recognised the red-haired man I passed in the street. We both turned round to look at each other, but neither had the courage to speak.

FIRST LOVE (2)

by

VAL WILLIAMS

I met him at the Youth Club - tall and solid, built like a young ox, with ginger hair. He had a rather shy, diffident manner which endeared him to me after the pushy, conceited males of my acquaintance. He was 17 years old and his name was Frank.

He bought me some squash and we soon started chatting, though perhaps I was the more talkative one at first. Our friendship blossomed slowly through weekly club meetings, trips to the cinema and lots of long cycle rides which we both enjoyed very much.

After one particularly long ride through the Kentish countryside, we stopped beside a cornfield.

"Come on," said Frank, "Let's have a rest here for a while, I'm sure the farmer won't mind."

We pushed open the unlocked gates, rested our bikes against the hedge and sat down on the edge of the field, flattening some of the corn as we did so. He lay back clutching a stalk and chewing it's stem as he went down. Then, placing his hands under his head, he stretched his bulk lengthwise and uttered a contented sigh.

"Come on Val, lie down as well, it's great."

My aunt had brought me up very strictly and I could imagine her disapproval at the idea of a young girl lying in a cornfield with an ardent young man.

"Oh no," I replied, "I'm fine sitting here - it's lovely."

Despite all Frank's protestations I remained sitting with my legs firmly crossed until we had to make tracks.

Another time out on our bikes we had just dismounted in a village at the bottom of a steep hill, when we heard shouting and clattering hooves We looked up to see a horse pulling a cart, rushing down the hill towards us - the driver was an old man - he was pulling at the reins and shouting at the horse to "Whoa !", with no avail. I expected Frank to rush forward and catch the reins and pull the poor frightened beast to a halt. I could see the headlines in the paper, "Local Boy Stops Runaway Horse - A Hero In Our Midst". To my disappointment, he just stood there and watched as the horse clattered by. Getting to the bend it stopped suddenly and the old man was thrown into the middle of the road. I then leapt into action.

"Stop the traffic, I'll look after the old man, he mustn't be moved in case he has broken something."

I had recently been to First Aid lessons and knew the drill. The old chap was groaning and obviously in a great deal of pain. I put my jacket over him and waited for assistance. People from the village arrived - one chap caught the horse, another called an ambulance and another directed the traffic until the village bobby arrived. Frank meanwhile stood around looking distinctly uncomfortable, his chance of being a hero in my eyes at least, was lost for ever. Eventually we remounted our bikes to go home. Reading the local paper the following week, we found that, sadly, the old chap had died a few days after the accident with a fractured pelvis.

Frank was a frequent visitor to our home and was always asked to Sunday tea - he never refused. One day he arrived in a new suit - green wool jacket complete with plus-fours and darker green long socks.

"I've also got some plain trousers to match," he said proudly. I suppose he chose green to go with his red hair, but why plus-fours - he didn't play golf ? He was sweating profusely and, to my eyes, looked ridiculous.

"It's very nice," I lied.

My aunt asked him, unkindly, if he would do a bit of weeding in the garden while she and I prepared tea. Always obliging, he went off to do his best without kneeling in his new trousers.

He eventually asked my aunt if she believed in early marriage ? Receiving a negative reply, we decided on a long engagement instead, as I was only 17. I expected a ring and I knew Frank was saving hard. One day he arrived at the front door full of excitement.

"I've got something to show you," he said.

"This is it," I thought, "my ring at last."

"Come outside," he said.

"Outside, " I queried, funny place to keep a ring. I went to the door with him and looked out. There, propped against the kerb was a *tandem bike!*

"I've bought this for us," he said, full of pride and excitement.

Needless to say, I was shocked and disappointed. It took a lot of persuading before I ventured out on that machine. It was a disaster from the start - sitting at the back with Frank's ample frame blotting out the view, I could neither brake nor steer. I paid him out though by not pedalling up the hills. He'd turn round at the top exclaiming how difficult it had been while all the time my legs had been propped upon the bar.

This tandem business was the beginning of the end. Frank had to go off and do his National Service and I started my Nursing Training. He came to say goodbye with the hope that we could still keep in touch ? I can still see the hurt in his eyes when I told him bluntly it was the end - my career would come first.

How sweet and how cruel can be "First Love".

Richard Kemp

CHAPTER THREE

Obsession

Obsession	**Jill Cocker**
Short Wave Girl	**Richard Kemp**
Star-Maker	**Richard Kemp**
Obsession	**June Lukins**
Obsession	**Val Williams**
Obsession	**Richard the Miller**

OBSESSION

by

JILL COCKER

I ran my hands over it again. The feeling rushed over me; it wasn't carnal it was far superior, it was anger and rage. I eventually replaced them in the drawer, but before I did I twisted them roughly between my hands and heard the delicate lace tear. I shut the drawer hard and crookedly on its runners. She wouldn't open that in a hurry, without tearing something else, and she wouldn't know I'd done it. I would leave her domain now. Two paces across the room, near the door, my hand was on the handle, then I saw it, the fragile glass candlestick. Stupid girl, leaving it casually on the floor still with the half candle. Bet she'd lit that when the boyfriend was here. I kicked out, the candle rose from my foot and hit the wall, smashing noisily. It was done. I heard a course laugh, I became aware it was from me. I could visualise her face, finding this, the fine skin, the large blue eyes, the long luxurious hair which glinted and gleamed as she moved. I could see pain in her eyes, despair and fear. I liked the fear, it filled me with strength. I'd teach her to turn me down again.

SHORT WAVE GIRL

by

RICHARD KEMP

The fine hairs at the top of her earlobe were brushing against the speaker as she adjusted the tuner. Jagged bursts of static, a distant humming note and peculiar whistling noises spiralled into the shell of her ear, her expression a running translation of sound. She could hear a voice, singing softly, storm-tossed on the ocean of short waves. The aural glimpses of the singer were visions of a tranquil melancholy, places where no one could visit. But the singer's voice kept moving about, as if nervous at revealing such personal Edens.

The voice eventually died under a whoop of atmospheric disturbance. The young woman, deprived of her dream, became increasingly frustrated. The radio burst in a wiry, plastic shower when she threw it at the far wall and fell onto the pillow of the unmade bed.

She sat by the window in the resentful silence of the dead radio. Outside, high up over the slick grey tiles of the houses, the ethereal singer was waiting. She needed a powerful, sensitive receiver and she decided to build it herself.

Later that afternoon, the young woman passed her landlord on the lower landing. He was mounting his customary guard over the stairs, his huge belly lounging against a stained shirt as he stood in the doorway. He eyed the cardboard box full of broken radios and library books on popular electronics which the woman was labouring with.

" I don't want any noise. Mrs Clayton will be complainin' if there's any noise ". She ignored him and hurried up the last flight of stairs, uncomfortably aware of the sharp glances that followed her.

She worked all night on the new receiver, hunched over the spidery circuit diagrams and dusty valves. She scrawled her plans on sheets of white paper that fluttered over the corpses of the dead radios, infusing them with new life.

She inserted the first component just after midnight, slitting her forearm precisely and forcing the small circuit board inside. The smaller components were embedded in her limbs with careful deliberation, the connecting wires spiralling over her pale skin. The speaker, a huge cone like a fly's eye, was melded just below the sternum, held in place by an intricate cradle of wires. The antenna took some time to adjust, but by threading the stiff metal under the skin of her temples, she found that the spiny structure could be supported with ease, around her head.

The new receiver was completed as the pale fingers of the new day caressed the window panes. The young woman plugged herself in and felt the surge of current race over her bloodied limbs. As the white noise of pain subsided, the voices began to fill the room. She moved about the small room, turning the tuner on her left shoulder, searching for the best reception. The speaker rattled in her chest as the sounds tumbled out and then the singer broke through, clear and sweet.

The woman stood by the window, the bird's nest of aerial shimmering about her head, as the melancholy music swept through her and around her. When the landlord hammered on the door, she just turned the volume up and closed her eyes.

STAR-MAKER

by

Richard Kemp

My grandfather was seventy-four years old and he liked collecting pieces of broken glass. I had to help him, because he couldn't get around like he used to, but I didn't mind. Grandma said I should have been out with other girls my own age, but I'd rather listen to grandfather talking about the energy of the sun and radio waves and other things.

Grandfather took me to school each morning. We walked through the park, not because it was quicker, but because there were always broken bottles on the path. Grandma clucked her tongue and grumbled about the hooligan element whenever she saw rubbish lying around, but grandfather knew its true value.

"The young rascal who smashed that bottle and ran off laughing with his friends has built a shrine to the sun", he would explain, as we examined our find.

He would hold his arms out to stop me treading on something important, his walking stick jiggling about in his hand. Knees bent, neck craned forward, he would peer intently at the tiny crystal fragments like a bird about to peck at a crumb. After a careful examination of the remains, he would carefully direct me to pick up a particular piece of glass. He was very fussy, but after a while I could guess which ones he would like best. They were quite large pieces, in triangles or squares. Sometimes we found the whole bottom of a bottle, which looked like a giant fish's eye, and grandfather would smile for the rest of the day.

Grandfather never told me what he was doing with the glass. He took the pieces from me and put them in a cloth bag he always carried. When we got home, he would send me into the house, while he went into the big shed in the corner of the garden.

He kept it locked and did not like me to go in there. When I looked through the window I could see bits of old radios, parts from motorcycles, bundles of wire and broken mirrors scattered over the benches. At the far end was a curtain of heavy green material which was always pulled right across. When I asked grandfather what he did with the glass, he would say "Oh, just experimenting with the nature of light, Susan. Perhaps I will show you someday," and then change the subject.

Last Saturday, as usual, grandfather was waiting by the front door for me when I came down. He was impatient to get started, so I had to hurry my breakfast, get dressed quickly and then we set out for the market square.

It was a clear, dry morning as we walked through the town, grandfather's short, quick steps hissing on the cracked and dusty pavements. We turned into the market square where three pubs look out over the neatly planted rockeries and herbaceous borders. Immediately, our practised eyes detected the glint of the morning sun on shattered glass.

Outside the Golden Grape we found three glistening sprays of powdery glass, even more beautiful to my grandfather's eyes than the flowers in the wooden tubs beside them. He looked carefully from every angle, but found nothing to suit his taste. Stepping carefully over the splashes of vomit we moved on to the Three Horse Shoes.

Here we found richer rewards. Several green beer bottles had been thrown against a wall. Grandfather was ecstatic, hopping from foot to foot , chuckling quietly to himself. He bent down, suddenly alert, and began to search amongst the scattered remnants for the ideal shape. He took his time, cautiously viewing from all angles, muttering about "refraction", "scattering" and "latent energies". Finally he chose three large pieces of dark green glass, still sticky, which I carefully picked out for him and put into the cloth bag.

We passed on to the Jolly Roger, but only one glass had been smashed there, and grandfather dismissed its crumpled form with a scowl and a twitch of his walking stick. He was unusually gloomy as we walked back home.

"Just one more piece to complete the puzzle, Susan. I hoped I would find it today, but it wasn't there. We shall look again this evening". His voice trailed away as he shuffled over the lawn to the shed.

We did not find the missing piece that evening or the next. Grandfather became increasingly agitated, grumbling to himself and stabbing the ground with his stick.

It happened yesterday as he walked me home from school. Grandfather insisted we go the long way, along Park Lane and through the churchyard. He was still looking for the missing piece of glass.

We stepped onto the cobbled pathways of the churchyard, my hand brushing some flakes of rust off the big iron gate. The trees were in full leaf, great oaks amongst the graves and slender poplars along the western edge. The graveyard was overgrown with tall grasses and brambles going brown in the hot summer sun.

We walked slowly, grandfather flicking the overhanging weeds aside with his stick as he searched among the cobbles. I got bored and ran ahead. I pushed my way through the long grass, which was dusty and crackled under my feet. I found my favourite gravestone amongst the brambles :

VICTORIA JANE
Aged 8
Who Fell Asleep
15th January 1887

It was leaning forward to the left and was covered with delicate feathery lichens of grey and green. As I looked solemnly at the gravestone, feeling a bit sad, I noticed the glint of broken glass amongst the withering weeds.

" Grandfather ! Grandfather ! I've found some!", I shouted. The old man stepped awkwardly through the tangled undergrowth, beating it down with his stick. I showed him the spot and he crouched and twitched his bird-like head over the remains.

"There!", he cried, pointing with his stick for me to pick it up. I drew the sharp fragment from the grass between finger and thumb, and held it out to the old man. He took it in his bony, twisted fingers and examined it with a keen eye. I saw it flash in the sunlight, a bright blue-white spark in his hand. He smiled at me and said "This is the last piece, Susan. My work is almost complete. Tonight, I will show you what this is all about.".

It was nearly eleven o'clock when grandfather tapped quietly on my bedroom door. I jumped out of bed and hurried to the door. My grandfather winked at me and put his finger to his lips.

"Don't wake your Grandma", he hissed, before we quietly went down the stairs.

Outside, the air was cool and still. The sky was orange over the town, gradually changing to dark blue then black high overhead, where the stars shone brightly.

We stood on the silvery lawn, staring up at the glistening stars.

"Wouldn't you like to live amongst the stars, Susan ?".

"No, Grandfather.".

He laughed quietly and said "That's good. You're young, you have many things to look forward to down here. But I am old and a little weary. I would like to join the stars tonight, and remain with them. Come along".

We walked over to the shed in the corner of the garden. The door was open and we stepped inside. The pungent smell of creosote and engine oil wrapped itself around me under a single naked bulb. The green curtain was drawn aside to reveal a peculiar machine, a wire cage, the size and shape of a man, wrapped in coils of copper wire which glowed a dull red. Surrounding the cage were many metal arms, jointed and twisted, on the ends of which were fixed the pieces of glass we had so carefully collected.

The splinters glittered under the harsh electric light. Grandfather grinned proudly and said,

"What do you think ?".

"It's very nice, Grandfather", I said.

"Wait until you see it working. Switch off the light and look the other way now, Susan, I have to get undressed, and you won't want to see me naked".

I did want to see him because adults look so funny without their clothes - like snails pulled out of their shells. But I did as I was told.

After a lot of shuffling about, Grandfather said "Nearly ready now, Susan". There was a clanging and scraping noise as he stepped into the machine.

"You must help me now, Susan. You must set me free. Do you see that lever, down by your feet ?".

I turned around and looked at the machine. Grandfather's wrinkled face peered out from amongst the twisting, glassy arms, his gnarled hands restlessly gripping the metal handles. I found the heavy iron lever.

"Push the lever down, Susan, and stand well back."

I leant against the lever until it began to creakily go down. As I pushed it to the floor, a skylight slowly opened in the roof of the shed. The silent starlight beamed in, and the mirrored machine sparkled in its shadowy corner. Each tiny sliver of broken glass had been arranged on its spidery arm to reflect onto another piece, so that a web of translucent white threads enveloped the machine. Grandfather was building a cocoon of light for himself.

Suddenly, I felt afraid for my grandfather, and shouted out to him.

"Don't worry, Susan", he called from within the humming threads of starlight, "I will always be there for you after tonight, you will never be lonely". There was a bright flash and sparks flew past my ears as I rushed into the garden. Looking back, I saw a deep red glow amongst the white threads as the copper coils began to murmur.

Roy Knowles

As the light got brighter, I moved back to the house. Brilliant white light poured from the shed door and windows, illuminating the hedges and washing lines. Grandfather's machine crackled and hissed, huge blue sparks bounced over the lawn like excited puppies. The noise increased, the deep humming notes seemed to vibrate in my chest, the pulses of brilliant light made me squint.

Suddenly, there was a moment's silence and the light dimmed slightly. I felt relieved and started to stand up. The shed exploded in a swirling ball of blue and white light. Bits of shattered wood and hot metal fell like hard rain, as I covered my head and sheltered against the house. When the noise, but not the bright light, had gone, I turned to the ruined garden.

Where the shed had been there was now just a blackened star shape on the grass, with a few ragged pieces of burnt wood glowing feebly. The machine was gone, scattered like a fallen satellite over the suburban gardens. But Grandfather was still in the garden, or rather over it.

He hovered ten metres up, arms flung out and an ecstatic grin on his face. He was immersed in light, it flowed in huge teardrops along his arms and fanned from his fingertips. Crackling white hoops of light flowed down his body and over his legs, expanding like ripples on a pond as they fell away from him. He began to float slowly upwards, leaving a misty, glittering trail in the air.

I stood in the garden and watched my grandfather shooting up to the stars on a comet's tail of fiery sparks. I knew he would be happy there, so when the neighbours began to cluck and chatter, I went quietly into the house.

OBSESSION

A Personal Glimpse

by

RICHARD THE MILLER

    Cap off

    Escaping Light
    Glimpse of Thigh
    Curval Bum
    Promises

    Alluring Smile
    Vein in Neck
    Liquid Eyes
    Sleight of Hand

    Rounded breast
    Dimp of Cheek
    Flexing Hip
    Reach to Touch

    Music Peaks
    Lips part
    Moisturing Tongue
    Closing In

    Dip Pink
    Raise to Ear
    Caressing Lobe
    Shivering

Commit Now
Wild Abandon
Is it Love
Who Cares

Punchy Climax
Between Love
And Madness
Lies Obsession

Obsession
By
Calvin Klein

Two Bob a Sniff

Obsession

by

VAL WILLIAMS

General house cleanliness was Ethel's obsession - in fact she had already got rid of two husbands with her remorseless and relentless pursuit of it. No time for relaxation in her time-table - up early with bed aired for one hour whilst she breakfasted, then dishes. In fact all dishes were washed and dried before the last mouthful of their contents were swallowed.

After breakfast the bedmaking was a ritual in itself. No modern duvet for her - white sheets and three blankets come summer or winter - the sheet had to be turned down an exact twelve inches. A silk counterpane was then spread over the bed for fear of a speck of dust falling on it.

Room cleaning was performed with absolute precision - everything was moved, dusted and put back in its place. Tables, chairs, window sills were dusted daily. Rugs were taken out and beaten within an inch of their lives. If a stray visitor were to sit on a chair or the sofa, the cushions were immediately plumped up as soon as the offending bottom was removed.

Every Spring she really came into her own - curtains were pulled down, loose covers dragged protestingly off chairs and the BIG WASH commenced.. Not an automatic washing machine for her :

"Those modern contraptions don't get clothes really clean," she grumbled.

No, she insisted on an old fashioned boiler with a hand wringer attached. As the sweat poured off her red face and her hair hung dankly down she was really happy. She felt in charge and in control - the boiling and bubbling of the "whites" gave her an almost sensual pleasure.

Another joy in her life was cleaning the silver and brass with which the house abounded. She'd collect all the small pieces on a tray and take them to the kitchen and begin her ritual - old white cloth to put the polish on, a navy one for the first polish off and then a final rub with one of the old vests. The newly shining pieces were then borne triumphantly back to their respective places.

And so life may have continued for Ethel until fate took a hand in the shape of a small black and white kitten which arrived one cold and wet evening. Ethel had opened the back door to fetch some more coal when the creature slipped in, mewing loudly.

"Shoo, shoo," she cried "I don't want your wet feet all over my clean kitchen floor."

The little cat would not be shooed and took refuge behind the old dresser, continuing to cry plaintively.

"All right - just one night, but you will have to go first thing in the morning."

She put some milk down for it and after a while the kitten ventured out and lapped it up greedily.

"You poor thing. I wonder where you've come from - someone turned you out I expect - there are far too many cats round here already, they chase the birds in my garden."

The little creature licked his paws, yawned, jumped up into the kitchen armchair, made himself comfortable and was asleep in a few seconds.

The next morning and the next and the next, Ethel shooed the kitten out, but it returned every evening for food. Eventually she allowed it to stay, it would jump upon her lap as she sat by the fire at the end of her busy day. It would purr - great rumbling sounds for such a small cat - then play with the end of her knitting needles, forcing her to lay them down and begin to relax. The cat grew bigger and became quite adventurous, he even climbed into Ethel's bed one day and wasn't shooed away. She enjoyed his company and talked to him all the time, calling him, "Marmaduke."

Subtle changes began to take place in the house, the bed wouldn't be aired until Marmaduke got up, dishes wouldn't be washed until the cat had finished his meals, the cleaning and dusting would be left so as not to disturb him. Even a slight film appearing on the silver and brass was ignored. Everything revolved around Marmaduke who grew big and fat with all the attention lavished on him.

As for Ethel she was really happy for the first time in her life - she even invited people in for a cup of tea - after all she could always talk about Marmaduke.

Marjorie St.John

Obsession

by

JUNE LUKINS

The announcer's voice crackled over the loudspeaker at the County Show.

"Would entries for class 42, Welsh Cob Stallions, four years old and over, please make your way to the collecting ring immediately."

A good number had already gathered there. Fine animals all in their glorious prime of life; fed, fettled and polished until they shone like satin in the midsummer sun. Their eyes and muzzles were smeared with baby oil to give a dark, dewy sheen and they had the traditional single plaited section of mane, just behind the ears.

Owners in open-necked shirts and with rolled up sleeves exchanged pleasantries, whilst at the same time summing up the opposition's chances against their own.

Others made their way in ones and twos from the lorry lines and stables situated a short way from the main ring, and a surge of spectators jostled for a view, where the crowd was rapidly becoming six deep. Everyone came to watch the cobs and decide where to send their mares to be covered next Spring,.

Then there was a hush as the crowd parted along the avenue ahead of a striking Liver Chestnut, not big, no more than fourteen and a half hands high, with four white socks and shimmering flaxen mane and tail.

He came meekly, behind the diminutive man in charge of him, occasionally uncertain where to put his feet and relying completely for directional guidance.

The others were now filing into the ring and responding to the cheers and applause of the crowd. They anticipated a thrilling spectacle at the end of the judging as the stallions would be "run out" at the furthest extent of their long reins, appearing to fly just above the turf of the showfield.

The Liver Chestnut's ears flicked back and forth, and he gathered himself up, as the man whipped the ancient towelling baby's nappy from the creature's eyes and stuffed it into his pocket.

Temporarily blinded by the sun, the horses nostrils flared as he shot into the ring and went immediately into the exaggerated snatch-extend, snatch-extend trot he had been trained to do, so beloved of cob enthusiasts everywhere.

The little man rattled the matchbox hidden in his palm and containing a few small objects. The sound caused the stallion to lift his feet higher and higher, remembering the searing pain of the long whip as it snaked along his belly, sometimes accompanied by the rattle when he and the man were alone. But not today.

Round and round they went, as the judge deliberated. Mustn't be rushed "My God this sun's hot" he thought, running his finger around the inside of the unfamiliar tight collar and tie.

"Hmm - the Big Black looks good today, he's matured well since last year and the Bay with the stockings has come on well too, but to my mind the Liver Chestnut's got it. Yes it's definitely his day today."

"Yes please steward, bring him in first, then the Black, the Bay and the Dark Palomino in fourth place."

The crowd went wild as the cobs were put though their final paces. Eyes wide, nostrils flaring and heavily weighted shoes drumming on the dry ground, round and round they flew. Out of the ring they fled and back into the horse lines, snorting with impatience and flanks heaving as they were rubbed down. Rugs were thrown over them and carefully fastened, as he cobs were settled to calm down. Then began the backslapping and inquests in the stockman's bar.

The merriment was well under way so no-one noticed the commotion around the Liver Chestnut's box, until the door of the bar flew open and in burst a teenage boy. It was then through the now-open door that the sound of the ambulance's siren could be heard as it threaded it's way through the crowds, and the enormity of what they all guessed was coming hit everyone.

The throng fell silent as the breathless lad collapsed sobbing onto the bench.

"The horse has kicked our dad in the head, he has. Reared right up and fetched those heavy shoes down on him, he did. He's in a real mess - our mam's gone in the ambulance with him, but it's a bad way that he's in. The bloody animal's still up in the stable, rampaging and trying to kick his way out he is. I can't find our Huw anywhere and I can't get near it myself. I've shut the top door before he kills someone, but I don't know what to do next and the din's awful."

In the peace and quiet of his darkened box, the Liver Chestnut calmed down and he stood now, head hanging, confused, exhausted and thirsty.

The public thinned out as the sun went lower and a steady stream of lorries queued to leave the showground. All except one. The low, alloy bodied one rumbled in through the gates. It drew up in the horse lines and the ramp was lowered outside the Liver Chestnut's box.

The talk in the bar was hushed now and the atmosphere sombre.

"Died at a quarter to four, he did - never regained conciousness. The lorry's here for the horse right now. Poor beast was crazed with fear of the man. Dai offered her and the boys a good price for him, to save his life. Dai always had a soft spot for him, and he'd have got him settled down and sorted out if anyone could. There was never any bad temperaments in his back breeding. They wouldn't hear of it though. That bloody man was obsessed with winning, he was, bloody obsessed !"

Chapter Four

Humorous

The Beast of Moorlake	**June Lukins**
Fluent Farsi	**David Browning**
Two Men, A Baby and a Rural Funeral	**Richard the Miller**

THE BEAST OF MOORLAKE
or
"Get that "thing" out of here right now !"

(As told by the Beast Himself)

by

JUNE LUKINS

I was looking for a good home on a farm with folks who didn't mind taking on a one-eared Norfolk Terrier dog pup, small perfectly formed and with a grudge against all that moved. Lugless Dugless - that was me. That was how I came to be whisked out of my warm little bed by the scruff of my neck, held up for appraisal and offered a job as a pest control officer. Then in a big smelly car I was driven away from my homeland and headed for some place called Crediton, where they speak a funny language.

"Snuggle him up in your lap", were my breeder's last words "so that he'll bond with you!!" She was dead right of course, I threw up going round the M25, and the missus and I were *nicely* bonded by the time we reached Devon.

After a few days I was introduced to a half-witted collie who legged it when I tried to be friendly. So now most of my days are spent trying to keep out of trouble myself and swing the blame for everything I do onto him. They say *he* hasn't got all his turnips on his truck, and *I* didn't know he could drive. Then I met some of the grandchildren - they ran away screaming too, perhaps it's my missing ear that does it, but it gives a chap a sense of power.

The missus doesn't mind though, she buries her nose in my neck and says I remind her of the seaside - all pees, poohs and rotten fish. Sometimes I get sent upstairs to get her up in the morning - she's not at her quickest then - but I soon shift her. She says it's like being hit round the face with a pair of kippers and someone letting loose a dozen gerbils under the bedclothes. It's an interesting thought, but I wouldn't know.

Lambing time here is fraught with risks for us dogs and we really have to pick our way around *very* carefully. Sneaking up on baby lambs is great sport, but with every little one comes a great big bad-tempered one who frowns and stamps her feet at us. I got trodden into the mud last year when I got surrounded by them and cornered. There are lots of little snacking opportunities though, and even the odd big banquet, if I can get a whole afterbirth to myself without old Garbage-Guts, the collie, noticing.

Which reminds me - I nearly overdid it in a big way last Winter. Was I ill ? I dragged myself out of bed. I'd had a terrible night. I forced open one bleary eye and ye Gods! In the corner of my kennel, a heap of intestines, no *surely* not, not *my* intestines. I was bundled into a plastic sheep food sack - oh! The indignity - but none wanted bodily contact with me in that state. Then I was whipped down to Mr Sylvie, the dog doctor and his partner Richard, who, shaking their heads said :

"Terrible bad way - not much chance. By the way - does he forage at all ?".

"Does he ever stop," muttered the Boss. Well I was grabbed - jabbed, stabbed - put on a drip and threatened with a bath if I ever got over it.

Missus is pretty good with all of us if we're poorly, but her methods *are* a bit unorthodox at times and you need to grit your teeth and hang on in there, as you never know what's coming next. Anyone of us could find ourselves dunked into a bucket of warm water, have a syringe full of glucose injected right by our tummy buttons, just the thought makes my eyes water. We might even get the hair dryer treatment and be bunged into the bottom of the Aga and told to keep our feet out of the rice pudding at the back. Ask the Boss, he's survived it for years - after a fashion. Says you can get used to *anything* if you've not much choice. I must say when she homes in on one of us, scoops us up with one hand, it's best to go with the flow so to speak, as it's an awful long way down again.

The neighbours here are pretty decent. If I can escape from the garden when Ed Parr goes down the lane to check his heifers and I run fast enough, he picks me up and gives me a ride on his tractor. He thinks I'm a damned nuisance really as he worries I'll get under the wheel one day. His dog Shep and old Garbage-Guts are really green with envy when they see me up there in the cab and what a revelation - it's a different world from six feet up, *my* eyes are usually only six inches from the ground.

Daphne's pretty good too and didn't even mind too much when the Pampas grass sprang into life in front of her and her horse's eyes - just as she drew level with it too!! That was the day I managed to slice a bit off my eyeball on one of the stems - so *down* to the dog doctor again!!

"Next time matey you're on your own," I'm told - so I've been a *lot* more careful lately, restricting myself to turning the compost heap over for mice, and a little light digging in the flower beds, and recycling the rubbish bags. Though they *say* there's little food value in eggshells, teabags and yoghurt pots, I have a lot of fun sticking them to my beard and eyebrows and frightening people who believe I'm the one eared chainsaw-toothed monster who comes up out of the drains.

Some of my relatives live nearby. There's Becky Beament who lives opposite and just about runs their place, and Buster Tucker at Beare Farm who's my Granpappy. He was not very impressed with me when we were introduced, as I haven't been around a lot yet - but boy has *he* lived! I hope I look like *him* when I get to his age.

I'd really like to go out on vermin control with the local lads and their dogs in the pickup truck, but the Boss says my colour is too much like the whiskery gentleman with the long bushy tail, and we can't afford more accidents.

Last week I ate the missus's pet toad and pee-ed on the chair leg. She said she knew it was me as Garbage-Guts aspires to much greater heights. Both little mistakes, you must agree, but she's said that the worst mistake around her is me, and that the next time we have a barbecue in the garden, I'm going to have a whole skewer all to myself. I love kebabs !!

FLUENT FARSI
(An Old Persian Tale)

by

DAVID BROWNING

In 1953 the Iranian Prime Minister, Mosaddeq, was toppled by the Army, with US backing, and the Shah was reinstated as ruler. The National Iranian Oil Company then issued a range of edicts to regulate the working practices of ex-patriate oil workers who were returning in great numbers. One such regulation stated that after one year, every foreign worker would have to take a test to show his proficiency in Farsi, the national language. Failure of the test would mean that their contracts would not be renewed.

When at the end of his first annual contract, a grisled, suntanned foreman pipelayer came to take the test, the examiner put the following question.

" If you want an Iranian worker to come here, what do you say ?"

Without hesitation the foreman replied :

"Bier Injah."

"Very good," said the examiner.

Then pointing to the far corner of the room he asked,

"What would you say if you wanted the man to go over there ?"

The foreman pondered long and hard, then quickly got up from his seat and walked to the far corner of the room and shouted,

"Bier Injah !"

The examiner awarded a pass but recommended that the foreman should work on his vocabulary.

TWO MEN, A BABY AND A RURAL FUNERAL

by

Richard the Miller

The telephone rang. Brother was on the line with some not totally unexpected news. Uncle George died in the early hours. Poor old uncle George. Not really. Uncle George was one of the great eccentrics, with his plus fours, copious consumption of good wine and whisky, and tales of adventure.

It was always a tale of adventure with uncle George. Even driving to the garage for petrol involved some side issue. People he saw, places he had visited, cars he had driven. It had always been cars with uncle George. As a motoring journalist he had been to every place where cars are exercised. Every launch worthy of attendance, all over the world.

Uncle George was to be buried near his home in North Cornwall. Time to ring our side of the family and gather the clan. Wife, unfortunately now garaged with a faster model, decided not to attend the funeral. No offence to George but whispering in the crypt might detract from the proceedings. Daughter with a ten-day-old baby understandably indisposed and second son unable to arrange time off. But eldest son accepted the rallying call and set off from London to arrive the night before.

Grandson, eldest son's son, is three months old and his mum has been in hospital since the birth. Not easy for her, not easy for baby living in hospital and not easy for senior son. So great efforts were made for baby to attend his first official social engagement with Dad and Granddad. New Dad, new Granddad and new Baby. None at all experienced in what was to come.

Son and grandson arrived at about eleven at night. Bottle feeding had taken place earlier and with much harnessing in the back the sleeping child had been whisked down the motorway. On arrival son announced that the little widget in his car said that the temperature was minus five. This information was to be of crucial importance.

Bottle feeding, baby bum care and general night provisioning all went off rather smoothly. Even saw the end of the late film. No noises during the night, all woke up at seven with sensible conversation and a deep, deep frost. The milk was frozen so both baby bottle and pint bottle were placed in hot water on the Rayburn. Cooked porridge, balanced baby in some sort of swivel apparatus that converts from car to dining room to baby carriage with one knobbly twirl. All very high tech!

The duck's water was frozen and while taking the dog for a walk his chilly paws lead to the realisation that baby wasn't really equipped for winter conditions. It appeared that the hospital was always highly heated and the contrast to Cornish moorland graveyard could be a problem. Where to get essentials in the time available? Urgent communication to daughter proved only marginally helpful. A call to a business colleague filled in a few gaps and we were advised that Boots is the place for mittens. We set off on the Great Mitten Hunt. Boots proved useless for chilly time clothes but we were directed up an alley to the mitten shop, camoflaged as a general female provision haberdashers. Hats of several shapes and hangers of unmentionables. Handsome mittens available in mock leather with a cord to go through the
sleeves. They look the part and although the thumb bit will not be filled for a year or two, they are destined to go down in family folklore.

Timing is everything for baby management. An hour to drive to the funeral, an hour for the funeral and then into the church hall for tea and stickies and a bottle of milk.

Feeding took a little longer than anticipated but no real problem and we arrived at the church thirty seconds before the hearse. Transformed the carrying contraption to a buggy on wheels. Met various relations briefly and then into the church before the procession started. At the porch a noble lady took down our details regarding relationship to the deceased. This was not anticipated so we involved her in working it out. The naming was straightforward but we then had nephew, great nephew and presumably great great nephew. It didn't seem quite right that a small child would be a great great anything so it was decided that George was his great great uncle. This was due to go in the press so we await a little artistic licence. There had already been one printed cock-up where George was described as an employee of the newspaper rather than a contributor and Aunt said it made it sound as though her husband had cleaned the drains.

We were ushered down the side of the middle pews with the baby carriage. Baby cuddled by father but not looking settled. Chanting was heard from outside as the vicar proceeded from hearse to church. Churches in North Cornwall are always built solidly, on rock and on a slope. No easy carry for the pall bearers. It was said that George lost a great deal of weight in the final days, for which four stout men were truly grateful. One of them my brother, who, being the eldest, struggled the most. Up
the aisle they traipsed, each holding the end of a rod attached to the coffin by a chain. Up the two steps towards the altar. Steady lads, steady. Lower slowly. Baby looked on. We all looked on as the bearers rejoined the congregation.

We sang a hymn. With only about twenty present, and the vicar playing the organ and being the only one who knew the song, we bumped along for six verses. 'Oh heavenly father help us' was chorused by all. Baby enjoyed the proceedings and started to whinney, not perhaps in tune but a positive contribution. The vicar prayed, baby whinneyed and we all said amen. We sat. Baby didn't approve. The vicar spoke of George. His ability as a communicator was praised. His great great nephew encouraged the vicar to speak up a bit. Emphasis was placed on George's war record and how the poppies had been left in the church for the funeral from Remembrance Sunday. This was too much because baby couldn't see the poppies. He could only see the backs of his relations in the pew in front. He decided to point out to the vicar the shortcomings of the proceedings from an infant perspective. The vicar had a cold, was losing his voice and failing to overcome the infant's challenge. Son rose, with grandson, and walked to the rear of the church. The vicar continued with anecdotes to raise the spirits. Baby raised his level of contribution. It was then that son made a tactical error.

Small Cornish churches are built to withstand the wind coming unhindered from the sea and the moors. The doors are heavily timbered, heavily hinged and have large wrought iron furniture. To try and open such a door with a baby under one arm is difficult. To try and do this without making a horrendous noise, from the hinges, the latch opening, the latch closing and the two pound round handle swinging back into position, is impossible. Great nephew and great great nephew had a grand exit and Uncle George could be heard laughing like hell. Or so I believe.

We sang some more and the service indoors being completed we watched the bearers latch on the carrying rods and the congregation processed to the graveside. Not unnaturally the new graves are the furthest away and up the steepest slopes. Eight granite steps slowed things considerably but eventually George was lowered into a grave dug out of soil and slate. The position was truly uplifting, overlooking the moors. The pall bearers held on to the vicar so that he wasn't blown onto the coffin. Physical damage during services is not an occupational hazard I would normally have associated with vicaring.

Aunt, a real trooper, broke down when encouraged to peer into the grave. Probably a good thing. One time when the stiff upper lip should droop.

We adjourned to the church hall where baby was applauded as the star of the show. Everyone drank tea. The older children ate and drank everything in sight, went outside to run about and then returned for more sausage rolls, sandwiches, cake, chocolate biscuits and buns.

Three generations of males on their first outing. No real problems and baby slept on the way home. All very pleasant, all very rural.

Barbara Aldridge

CHAPTER FIVE

2050

2050   June Lukins
2050   Jeff Kingaby
2050   Jill Cocker
2050   Rachel Maggs

2050

by

JUNE LUKINS

The elderly woman climbed slowly, stiffly onto the rock ledge and squatted there. A silent ghost-like grey dog slid around a boulder and sat companionably beside her. She had been coming here regularly since she was old enough to remember. It had been her own special place, with space and time for thought - but today was a special day for the inhabitants of the plain spread out below her. Her hand gently stroked the silver and turquoise ring that had been her mother's and she thought of her childhood and teens at the end of the previous century, and the poverty and squalor they had endured on the hopelessly overcrowded reservation. The average life expectancy then had been 50 years and intruders had a higher chance of being killed by the drink and drug crazed driver of a pick-up truck than by an arrow a hundred years previously.

Her gentle family had spent their winters in a shack, fashioning the beautiful "Eagles feather" jewellery that they sold around the Summer fairs and Rodeos, although it had depressed them to think of a symbol that represented freedom and had been theirs through history, being worn against the pallid skin of tourists. Now it was different - the herds of black/brown buffalo were increasing every spring on the higher plains, and directly below, a large and successful settlement had grown, with industry, schools and a hospital. The lower plains grew grain and a steady stream of trucks transported goods all over the states.

She had now seen so much change. Her husband had died the previous winter, but she had the comfort of her two sons who were on the Indian council, with her daughter, who was a successful lawyer. A clutch of grandchildren visited her every day and begged her to tell them stories of the past and teach them some of the old ways. There was also the knowledge that theirs and other tribes were increasing in numbers with every decade as true blood Native Americans were finding their way home from far away places. The big changes had come about when more and more of the world's population had become aware, and were concerned at their tragic history. Campaigning groups had pressurised the US. Government into finally, reluctantly, admitting its guilt in violent human rights abuses of its native population over many years.

It had taken until that day in 2025 - exactly twenty five years ago, for an agreement to be signed, handing back the plains they had occupied for many hundreds of years, and where the souls of their dead had borne witness to the injustice and carnage. The many millions of dollars in compensation would help with more development in future, and although in her heart she was saddened that it had come too late for her and her generation, she was filled with hope for those who would inherit these beautiful plains.

2050

by

JEFF KINGABY

'Dinners ready Pete'
Pete ignored his wife and continued browsing his computer screen, examining the giant redwoods on the west coast of British Columbia.
'Look dear. Look at the size of those trees they're the....'
'Yes Pete. But I said dinner's ready'.
'Sorry dear, got quite carried away'.
He took a paper plate containing several cheese sandwiches.
'Sandwiches?'
'I have been too busy to make a proper meal. Got to rush. I have a meeting in Paris in five minutes'.
Pete examined his sandwich, asking :
'What sort of day did you have Pet?'
'Had a lovely day in London. Saw Lord Microsoft arrive from California. Do you know his jet landed on the palace lawn? They've extended it quite a lot to take this huge 797'.
Realising the sandwich was better than nothing Pete took a bite, then said :
'A man in San Francisco told me it cost him 300 billion Europounds. Suppose it would if you bought up half of Belgravia. I wonder what the Queen thinks of it. They say she's happy living in Barbados.'
Tavvy interrupted : 'And I looked at those marvellous dresses in Harrods. There was an evening gown there for four hundred thousand Europounds. Still, what do I need new clothes for?'
Her mind wandered as she imagined herself entering the large ballroom of Microsoft Palace dressed in that wonderful evening

gown. She smiled as she was being introduced to the great man. Then remembering she was in her flat, she sighed.

'What sort of day did you have Pete? Apart from your experiences in British Columbia?'

'Spoke to an Aussie in Adelaide about the gum trees. Do you know they're absolutely marvellous. They actually grow stronger after they have been burnt in a forest fire. Had a look at the suburbs of Delhi, first time I've seen them. This afternoon I bought some shares in that new Mail Order Company at the Stock Exchange. Checked the bank account at Maidstone. By the way we are not overdrawn after all, thank goodness. Looked at the new 986 computers in Tokyo and finished up in British Columbia.'

'Sounds interesting Pete. Sorry must go. I have a marketing meeting with the woman in Paris.'

She returned to her study, sat at the desk, examined the computer screen and started tapping the keyboard.

From his flat on the 32nd floor Pete stared down into Crediton High Street. All the shops were closed and boarded up, the only movement was a solitary delivery van. It was early evening and not another soul in sight. He cast his mind back to the days of traffic jams, busy airports, bustling shopping centres and crowded trains.

'I wonder what sort of day Lord Microsoft had?'

2050

by

JILL COCKER

Kellum pulled down his visor and heard it click shut against the armour of his space suit. He no longer smelt the gas. His father, Dwight, said this would happen.

"You will have lost your sense of smell by 25." he'd predicted.

What he hadn't said was that he'd also lose taste too. Not that it mattered, he had moved on to the over-25 pills range and they all seemed the same. He was thinking this as he slid his body into the driving seat, pulling by his hands. No one used their legs these days. From age 15 you lived in your own spacecraft in the atmosphere. Back in 2010, when some people still lived on earth, a nuclear war happened between two large organisations from a little country known as Great Britain. The people from this country were supposed to have greater brains than anyone from anywhere else. Kellum thought, less brains really, to let two organisations have so much power.

His birth, after that time, was considered miraculous. Most people lost their ability to reproduce. Dwight and Kylie had been on their honeymoon at the time when Kellum had been conceived, orbiting Venus, and out of deadly range.

Kellum's mind reverted to his present mission. His parents would be so angry when they found out. He risked everything. But it was his last chance to see it and to get some of it. If he could have his own child he could pass on this experience. It felt so important to him.

Gathering speed he switched off his VDU screens so that he could concentrate wholly on the control panel in front of him. The green lights flickered, reflecting some strange siver-green patterns on his light space suit and a red light under a small VDU flashed angrily. That was Kylie wondering why he was not receiving her. He ignored it.

Soon he entered the earth's atmosphere and the black smog in which the earth was always blanketed. He flicked a switch and his autoray map and radar appeared. He zoned his target. The putrid oily atmosphere was thick and impenetrable to all but the shortest vision. The map light started to flash. In his space suit Kellum sweated. Nearly there, nearly done. His ambition almost complete. Then he saw it. His breath was coming in short rasps. There it was, the only known one left. It stood barely alive and wearily outstretched over burnt barren earth. He put the craft to hover halfway down this lovely creation. He could hardly believe that they had once almost covered the earth, for anyone to touch and admire.

Kellum found he was crying with emotion. He opened the window and grabbed. He'd got some! The small opening snapped shut within seconds and Kellum's shaking elongated fingers held his prize.

But the damage was done and his clinical atmosphere was now a choking black cloud. Two breaths and he'd turned the craft, feeling the insidious effects already of the pollution, through all his protection, penetrating his sensitive sterile lungs. The craft, on autopilot, was shooting back, but Kellum lay, his breathing laboured. His trophy, a small wizened acorn attached to a tiny oak leaf, lay in the open palm of his hand.

2050

by

RACHEL MAGGS

When she went to get the eggs that morning there were no chickens left. She stood staring into the depths of the hen house, somehow expecting at least one to appear. The caustic chickeny smell finally brought her round and she stumped back to the shelter.

"Weren't no corn left, anyway."

It was quite light inside - her one grimy pane faced east. They had gone in that direction, would return from it, and that was where she looked to. You could see the smoke and glow from the boundary road, but the more you stared the nearer it seemed to get, and the noise of guns played tricks on your mind as well - on and on, louder and louder, overlaid with sudden shouts and cries and screams. But that wasn't right.

"Pushing them back all the time," the radio had said until it stopped working. Probably not as fast as they thought at the beginning - but pushing them back all the same - back where they came from.

She sat in the deck chair nearest the unlit burner, glanced at the over-familiar squalor and carried on with her letter.

"And now all the hens is gone," was added to her list of complaints. Quite how or where this letter was going to be posted did not concern her just now. Why had they not been back since the morning they left grim faced and armed ? She had waited up for them, cooked dinner as well until the food started to run short. And how much longer would that last ?

"I don't know how long I can carry on here. I've not seen a single soul for I don't know how long, the radio broke last week, you ought to come home and help when you're needed. From your loving mother."

The letter had ended rather abruptly, unwelcome thoughts were surfacing. She hadn't seen or heard from anybody, but somebody must be about to have taken the chickens. Perhaps someone had found the shelter and been in there as well - broken the radio perhaps.

"No, no. No-ones been here because no-one don't know where 'tis."

She started at a noise, it sounded like chickens' feet scratching the corrugated iron. That was it ..... she'd forgotten to lock them up ! She went out to look - she could hardly breathe - the air was thick and rotten. But the guns ! The guns had stopped. The silence pressed on her and the fires in the east choked her with their rancid smoke. So close. So close. She turned to run back to the shelter and saw the edge of the iron door closing down. They were back. It was over. They were back.

Silhouetted against the fiery eastern window, fiddling with something, a familiar figure.

"It's broke," she said. A foreign face looked up at her words, a foreign voice suddenly blared from her radio. It was over.

Chapter Six

It should never have happened here

It Should Never Have Happened Here   **Rachel Maggs**
It Should Never Have Happened Here   **Jill Cocker**
It Should Never Have Happened Here   **Richard Gard**

IT SHOULD NEVER HAVE HAPPENED HERE

by

RACHEL MAGGS

His screams rang out across the shop-floor. Clearly audible above the racket of the machines, it took us all a few seconds to take in what was happening. Locating the source amidst such a clamour of noise was hard enough, but the unreality of the sound itself slowed us all down.

By the time we saw him it was too late. The lad on the lathe next to him had finally run over and hit the emergency shut off, but the rest of us were rooted to the spot - mouths open, hearts pounding, oblivious of time. Our machines continued operating - turning, milling, grinding, drilling - but we ... we were transfixed, mesmerised by the final lazy rotations of his chuck. A flap of blue overall, like a flag, waving coyly from the jaws.

Suddenly an instructor appeared and slapped the red button on the wall. All our machines stopped simultaneously, deprived of power, and the dying whines of heavy gears echoed into silence.

"Stay where you are !"

The panicky edge of the instructor's voice jarred us back into real time. They were all out of the office now, heading down the gangway.

"Hold on lad !" In an undertone, "What's his name again ?"

We were all starting to fidget - looking round at each other. The spell had been broken and we became awkwardly aware of our

isolation. The shock was too great for sixteen year olds; we needed to huddle together, sharing the experience - but none of us dared move. At last an ambulance came. The scrum of adults around him grew denser - and we all thought for sure he was dead. They had to put his lathe in reverse to wind him out of it - I thought I heard some unworldly groans - but finally they took him away.

The power was turned back on later that day; his machine started up again as if someone was standing there idly spinning the chuck. The flapping piece of overall had to stay there until the safety officer had inspected it, so did the clumps of ginger hair and blood stains leading to the door. It was a horrible reminder and we all avoided it.

By the end of the week, though, it had passed into our collective history. Sick jokes abounded and we all found our own way of forgetting it. And when he turned up, months later, it was as if we'd never really known him. It was very busy and noisy that day. No one had a chance to talk to him, and in the workshop he started shaking - his Mum had to take him home. Someone said he was crying. He should never have come back - it was embarrassing.

We never saw him again.

IT SHOULD NEVER HAVE HAPPENED HERE

by

JILL COCKER

Jim bent down, put out his finger and touched the red sticky mass that was oozing towards him. It looked like gallons and gallons but a body only contains eight pints he thought to himself, there can't be any more than that, even if she was left empty. His mind felt completely still. despite the pandemonium around him. Officer Green pushed roughly past him, ashen, shock and horror had drained the blood from his face. Jim had only seen him with chin jutting, sneering, power happy. But now he looked weak and frightened, almost flimsy. I'll never be scared of him again, he thought.

Pushing his back further into the small space between the door jamb and the bars, Jim watched compulsively while the doctor, who had followed Officer Green, stood up from the body and shook his head.

"She's gone, I'm afraid." he said.

Jim heard the laboured progress of the ambulance crew clattering through the broken debris that had been the school room. They quickly cleared a path and then a space. The stretcher was lowered. The doctor looked up from his conversation with officer Green.

"Too late, she's a gonner. Photos and then you can go."

More people were cramming noisily into the room. Jim was the only inmate left.

The click and the flash. They were gone. The noise from the cell block was subsiding. Jim wondered if Bomber had left anything unbroken in the cell he shared with him. The tension in the building was stifling, he couldn't breathe. He quietly moved his cold limbs. His teeth were chattering.

He was catching some of the general remarks. "What on earth possessed him?" and "He won't get out of this." "The Guv'nor was there too. Bet he's thinking about his job!"

Benny wasn't a psychopath, how could he be? Jim thought. She must have put pressure on him to talk, more than he could bear, he was OK if you just left him alone. He talked to the models that he carved and he even had names for them. I know, thought Jim, inspiration suddenly coming, she must have taken his model away. That's what had done it.

"Well there is nowhere but prison now to send the likes of these psychopaths." The Guv'nor's cultured but exasperated voice drifted across. "What tool had he kept back? Why wasn't it noticed?"

Officer Green approached him, "Right Jim" he said "Or is it Benny today?" The sneer was back on his face as he spoke. "Into solitary for you, probably for ever."

Jim hauled roughly from his hiding place, walked awkwardly, his wrists tightly cuffed.

"It should never have happened here." He said to the officer. "I should have waited 'til I was out, I'd got her address."

IT SHOULD NEVER HAVE HAPPENED HERE

by

RICHARD GARD

I heard the wail as I was feeding the calves. The sound seemed to vibrate off the metal sides of the milking parlour across the yard, but the calves hardly noticed the racket and guzzled the milk.

From the calf house I couldn't see the road so it might have been a fire engine or an ambulance, I'm not sure that I know the different noises they make. I heard a car pull up in the lane that passes through the farm, but I didn't concern myself. The calves needed doing and if someone wanted me they would holler. That's how we go on, if you want someone, shout! Tom, my husband, is over at Malcolm's getting a part welded. The sound of someone running across the concrete yard carried into the calf house but it wouldn't be my husband. My menfolk never run, well not in the middle of the afternoon on a hot summer's day.

"Is anyone about", a voice called, urgent, worried. I stepped out of the calf house and saw a man in a tie calling as he ran. I recognised him as a rep from one of the feed firms. Phillip his name is and I've always found him very pleasant. He saw me and stopped. I will never forget the distress on his face as he fought to say those terrible words, "There's been an accident". My God, you always live with this in farming. I knew, I just knew one of mine was involved. "It's in the village, I'll give you a lift" he offered.

Phillip's car was a new rep's car with mobile phone and clips to hold messages. I remember apologising for my wet trousers and boots, where the calves had spilled the milk, but I knew he wasn't bothered about that. Not today, maybe at another time but not today.

He had been driving through the village, when he was stopped by the police. He saw the ambulance and a handful of people. He saw a tractor, parked beside the road, and he saw a trailer loaded with straw at a strange angle against a garden wall. He saw Hugh, my nineteen year old son, sitting in a police car. Tony White, the local community policeman, was standing beside the police car talking into the radio and Phillip thought he had better find Tom or myself or both. He didn't use his mobile phone and I've never asked him why. Some things just have to be done face to face. Better that way, much better, for me, as it turned out anyway.

What happened when I stepped out of the car I remember vividly. We count Tony as a family friend and he put one arm out to guide me. We didn't touch, it wasn't a greeting, just a shield almost, a gesture of support and protection. The police car door was open and Hugh stood out to hold on to me. He hadn't done that for a long time, but we hug regularly now. Mutual support in times of difficulty, even very minor things like me getting to the teapot when the men have drunk it all, silly things I suppose, but how I welcome those contacts.

Clearly Hugh was not injured. He blurted out about the trailer becoming unhitched. Nothing he could do, it swerved across the road. My mind became cold. Who? The ambulance. And then Mary came over. Thank God for Mary from the post office. Her husband died from cancer and she took the post office to keep her busy. She knows everyone but never tittle tattles. The sort of woman who is strong. Strong inwardly. She would find 2,000 tents and 10,000 blankets in an emergency, I'm sure she would!

"Who"? I said.

"It's young Angela Crouch" said Mary. "She was standing by the wall talking to her mother when the trailer hit her".

Angela used to be very active with the Young Farmers before she was married and I know Angela's mother Beryl very well. Beryl and I made cakes for the village fete last month. She is such a likeable person with an infectious laugh and so looking forward to her first grandchild. Dear God, the baby. Angela was due in a few weeks. Mary looked me straight in the eye.

"She's dead" she said, "Mr Norris got to her in seconds, but there was nothing he could do, poor man, she died instantly, no pain."

I don't know Mr Norris very well. He moved into the village a while ago having been in the army. It turned out he was on his way to the post box.

"And Beryl ?", I pursued.

"Dr Williams is with her now but she's not hurt, no broken bones", replied Mary.

The next few days passed and the police came to the farm several times. They and the health and safety people examined the tractor and trailer. One of them said that it could have been hitched up wrongly. Since the tragedy Tom and Hugh have gone over and over the way the tractor was used that day. All day it had been carting straw. All day. How can it be hitched up wrongly? How come it didn't separate earlier. How, how, how?

We all visited Beryl and her husband Cliff, and John, Angela's husband. We couldn't say the right words and left sooner than we thought we would. I see Beryl now but the sparkle isn't there. I know she doesn't blame us, but it was our trailer. Hugh hasn't said much. Quiet by nature he keeps things to himself. I know he cried and I know that he talks to John Crouch.

Two months later Hugh came back from Tuckers, the agricultural engineers, with a long strop of steel and he wraps that around the tow hitch everytime he takes out a trailer. Tom now does the same, and so do our neighbours, since the letter.

I've never really understood about research. Things are written up in the farming press and we get no-end of leaflets. Tom had been heard to comment that people do research instead of an honest day's work, but he doesn't say that now. Not since the letter. Not since Hugh saw the article in the paper about the project looking into tractor accidents and I wrote, just on the offchance, to see if there had been other incidents. I don't know what I expected really, but back came the information that trailers unhitching are not uncommon, and details of how.

When that letter arrived I have never seen Hugh read something so carefully. He put it aside and read it again. He didn't say a lot at first but he and Tom spent time in Broad Meadow and borrowed extra chains from Tuckers. Now we know. One stupid, silly, spring. One spring to hold several tonnes. We never recognised the risk and we have to carry on. Those researchers have to solve the problem. The ambulance must not wail near other farms next summer.

Chapter Seven

Justification

Justification	Rachel Maggs
Justification	Sharon Gill
Justification	June Lukins
Justification	Richard Gard
Justification	Jill Cocker

Justification

by RACHEL MAGGS

She shot out of her chair like an ejected pilot, and was at his desk shouting in his face before he - or she - knew what was happening. The change from demoralised self pity to raging aggression had taken a frighteningly short time. She had worked for this guy for four years and had always calmly accepted what he told her, until now. Shaking with anger and humiliation, all the frustrations of the last months poured out in a surprisingly lucid stream of abuse. He tried to stand up, but she was leaning so far over his desk he couldn't get out. He must have wondered if she was going to leap over and grab him by the throat - it was his terrified expression that finally got through to her. She flopped back into her chair exhausted - shocked that she had lost it like that.

He had adopted a soothing tone, but whatever it was he was saying washed over her. She left the office with no memory of what had finally been agreed, and having pulled the door shut behind her, lent back against the cold metal trying to collect her thoughts. The expectant silence and carefully averted eyes told her that the whole building had shared her enraged outburst. She couldn't return to her desk as if nothing had happened; it wasn't home time, but she got her things and walked out.

She didn't know what to do next, and ended up just sitting in her car. Her hands hurt, and she found neat rows of bloodied half moons across the palms. She sat staring at them - sort of laughing and all the while sniffing back the tears. Trying to replay what had happened - trying to rehearse what would happen next. Her lips were moving. A panicky wave started creeping over her. "I can't go home. I can't go home."

The thing was - she knew what her husband would say. He'd been telling her all along, and she chose not to hear it. But she couldn't leave her home every day for a job that meant nothing. She had to justify it to herself, and it just didn't make sense unless she had a brilliant career, and that was what she'd been promised. Brilliant prospects if she could just prove how committed she was in this immediate post-natal period. And it had suited her fine because when it came down to it, she didn't want to be at home immersed in nappies and milk. If it meant giving up feeding the baby to do night shift, OK. If it meant going away for a week to be the team leader for the remote installation, OK. It was all easy for her to justify because there was a carrot at the end of it which would benefit the whole family. Money. Money for schools, money for mortgages. But the carrot, the promotion, the pay rise, the glory - wasn't there. It had never been there - never been hers to promise them - there had been no justification at all.

People were starting to look in at her. She had to get away - drive off somewhere, anywhere. Mad thoughts assailed her. Could she crash the car and avoid having to tell him ? Stay at a hotel, disappear ? Nothing made sense, and before she could think of another destination she was turning into he own drive. He was in the garden and turned, smiling to greet her.

"You're early." She'd forgotten about the time. "What happened, then ? Did you see him ?"

"I don't.......I can't talk about it just now."

She was looking at her feet, but she could feel the patronising sympathy and disappointment oozing out of him. The in-drawn "Oh," the sighed out "No." The told-you-so intonation.

She walked away from him. She couldn't listen to it. She felt fragile and brittle. She walked precisely along the path, into the house, closed the door carefully and walked upstairs. She felt like she might break.

He found her staring into the cot. He couldn't understand what she was saying, and he had to turn her face to him to see her lips. The look in her eyes was frightening to him - but he finally made out what she was saying. "She's not a baby any more."

Justification

by Sharon Gill

Where does justice appear in my life ?
Does it abandon in trouble and strife,
Or is it the sword that cuts the cord,
The judge who sits on almighty throne and decides my fate ?

How does justice touch my soul ?
Fearfully !
My wrongs to be punished,
An angry father condemning blameless curiosity.

A date with Karma as the wheel turns again
And the same mistakes are made.
Guilt subsides and the wheel stops spinning,
New thread is woven,
Justice is beginning.

Nothing is left unjust.
There is always a toll of sadness and anger
Relieving our knotted and painful state
And all our self hate,.

To open a brighter doorway,
It's okay to cry,
Anger can be transformed.
It is so upon the larger wheel of life,
Acceptance our key through the brighter doorway.
It is so,
Just so,
It is just.

Justification

by

JUNE LUKINS

Dear Santa Claus,

    Greetings to yourself and Mrs Claus, I hope you both enjoy good health. I wonder if you can see your way clear this year, to bring me a trailer to tow behind my motorbike ? It doesn't HAVE to be a big one.

    I wouldn't normally ask for myself, but the dogs, Dan and Duggie have expressed the desire to attend Motorcycle Rallies and as neither has passed his test yet, it would come in very handy for transporting them and their gear.

    I realise that you are rather pushed at this time of the year - but a nice upside-down goldfish bowl type turret on the top would enable Dan to see where he is going, as he gets rather nervous about nasty surprises, and a letterbox slit at the back with a sign saying "rear gunner" over it would suit Duggie to a "T" as he likes to see where he has been.

    Perhaps you could airbrush a nice skull in a top hat over the side for us. We'd like that quite a lot. I feel sure that this would be a better long term option than buying a succession of new kennel doors for Dan as he eats the bottom of his in frustration at being left behind.

    It would be helpful, too, to have their guidance back to our own tent late at night, as we have on occasion got it wrong, to the acute embarrassment of all concerned. They all look the same in the dark you see.

    You must surely agree that the slight difficulty you may experience when you come to deliver it would be well justified when you consider the obvious benefits. I will await the delivery and the fall of soot with gleeful anticipation........

Justification

by

Richard Gard

AMBIOS System configuration
Boot up
Wait

Systems check
Expanded Memory OK
Virus Search
Windows
Automenu
Leaves
Program Manager
WordPerfect
Document Unmodified
Click File
Open
How Titled ?
Home Directory
Writing
Just.doc
Read
Layout

Visual appeal
Page or Document
Click Document
Margins
Not Marginal
Centre
Too Odd
Auto Left
Click Right
More Odd
Straight Line Left
Straight Line Right
Full Justification
Save
Print
Full Doc
Exit.

JUSTIFICATION

by

JILL COCKER

Charles put down his pen and rubbed his eyes, dislodging his glasses and leaving them resting on his nose at a peculiar angle. He didn't notice. Burning the midnight oil yet again was stretching him over and above the limit, and his clarity of thought and concentration were definitely suffering. The cursor on the screen in front of him flickered and irritated his tired vision. The rows of digits on the sheets beside him on the desk were just a blur. Despite all, however, the golden triumph of achievement shone through. This was what it was all for.

He hardly dared breathe as he pressed in the last command sequence that he had been working hard on for so many months. The end was in sight, another flicker from the screen and suddenly it began from the top of the text, each line spacing itself equally. Almost a miracle. He watched enthralled. He wanted to share this moment with someone. He remembered his life apart from his work, totally empty. But it wouldn't be from now on. He would be the man of the moment, definitely the Programmer of the Year 1977, with abundant social opportunities. As he crossed the floor, fumbling for his keys, he thought with irony, I will call this new function "Justification."

Chapter Eight

No Particular Place to Go

Magnus	**Richard Gard**
A Glass of Water	**Richard Kemp**
Untitled	**Sharon Gill**
KGB	**David Browning**

Magnus

by

Richard Gard

Total trust as I held the elbow in a bent forward position.
The syringe emptied.
As my friend sagged I laid him down slowly, not wanting to let go.
Unnaturally asleep, his eyes open and staring.
I passed my fingers over the lids but they wouldn't close.

The stethoscope was pressed into the chest hair
No heart activity detected.

For nearly seventeen years we have enjoyed each other's company.
Active memories.
Of course I'll miss him, but I'm not too troubled.
A good life and I was able to prevent too much pain.
The least I should do for a true friend.

A GLASS OF WATER

by

RICHARD KEMP

The man sat silent and still, his hunched shoulders sending a gracefully arched shadow onto the grimy kitchen floor. The sunlight poured thick and golden into the dusty room, leaving the corners in blue shadow. The dancing motes of dust settled reluctantly amongst the fine hairs on the man's head, as his thoughts danced frenziedly beneath.

The man stood up, the rickety wooden chair scraping its splintered legs across the floor. Stealthily, he wiped a dirty glass with his shirt and filled it with water. He held the full glass to the sunlight as a jewelled offering, before carefully placing it on the table. He then opened a paint-chipped drawer and selected a large kitchen knife; not very sharp, rusty even, but sufficient for the task in mind. He placed the knife beside the glass, then carefully removed his drab, crumpled clothes. He savoured the feeling of freedom as the few garments he wore were thrown onto a chair. His pale skin glowed in the cool, shadowy kitchen. He looked down at the table and tried to decipher the delicate diffraction patterns thrown by the glass of water. The message became clear and he took up the knife.

Placing the tip of the knife carefully at each starting point, he made a series of incisions in the gaps between his ribs, six deep red petals on each side. The grey tissue of his lungs exuded through several of the cuts, although there was little bleeding. Metamorphosis had already begun. He put the knife down and stepped up onto the chair, turning awkwardly to face the glass of water. He felt his throat constrict as he began to take the air directly into his lungs. Suddenly, the man bent at the knee, lowering his shoulders, then leapt high up, his head brushing the naked light bulb as he curved over and down. He felt himself hanging in the air, time slowing down as his body changed. He felt each atom in his body shift, as myriad shapes and colours filled his mind. The yawning mouth of the glass widened with each new shift, the glass mating with the sunlit air to envelop the diving man.

The water wrapped itself around him like a living cloak. He twisted and writhed as his arms shortened and splintered, the flesh becoming web-like. His legs folded over each other and melted into one muscular limb, the toes fanning out like peacock's tails. His skull stretched out over his back, the eyes bulging and moving to the side. His jawbone thrust forward to a point and the change was complete.

He was swimming in the dark at first, getting used to the rhythmic movements of his new body. After some time he saw light above him. Shadowy forms, reassuring, swam beside him. Others like him, swaying in the warm currents, the sunlight playing over luminous patterns of green, red and yellow on their sleek sides. He was just below the surface now, dazzled by the wavy reflections.

The man rejoiced in the sleek muscularity of his new form. He wriggled his tail and felt the rushing waters on his bulbous eyes, the surging current in his mouth and through the sensitive gills. To the left and right, above and below he could see others like himself, silver teardrops dappled with crimson. He sensed that he was one cell in a living whole, one vital part of a single pulsating organism.

He leapt with the others when they reached the churning waterfalls, the oxygen rich water acting as rocket fuel to power him upwards, rainbow colours dancing in the dazzling air. He felt unstoppable, a driven thing, racing onwards to the head of the river.

The river became narrower, the other fish closed in around him, his world a chaos of fins and skeletal tails, glittering scales and eyes like black beads. The closeness of the other bodies caused a heated lust to rise in him, something in his belly boiled and set his body on fire. Faster and faster he raced, the last heart-bursting effort before death-that-gives-life.

The river opened out into a shallow lake. He could feel his bone-white belly touch the slimed pink rocks and gravel. The mass of fish slowed to a standstill, bloated bodies slid over one another. As

his eyes broke the surface he felt the hot sun on his back. Tendrils of thick, white seed fell from his body. The very life seemed to spill from him, his gills straining in the over-crowded waters.

He could feel his used up flesh bloating in the warm water. On all sides, fish twisted feebly, rising on the backs of others before flopping back exhausted into the morass. His sensations contracted as nerve endings died. His life imploded to a single white point behind his eyes.

But he did not die. The tiny seed of his existence swelled and put out roots. The dead cells of his body were rearranged, shifted into elegant new patterns. An intricate structure of bones, sleek powerful muscles, forests of delicately branching feathers. The blood surged through his new heart, air filled the lungs and with frantic beatings of his new wings he clawed himself into the air.

The startled black discs of his eyes were exposed and he took in the scene below, where a reef of dead and dying fish flashed scarlet in the sun. But he was free, rising on broad wings into a bright sky.

Looking left and right he glimpsed the elegant curves of his wings which stroked the air in deep, slow sweeps. The feathers were blue and green and the sun formed ever-changing silver webs of reflection as the wings spread out, beat downwards, then folded and rose to beat once more.

He rose giddily on the warm air currents, the landscape opening out below him. The green hills swelled and dipped, soft blankets of grass over sleeping giants. A haphazard geometry of hedgerows and woods divided up the green country. He flew higher and plunged into the moist embrace of galloping white clouds, emerging into the clear air, then turning and diving in once more.

Rising and falling, sweeping to left and right, he revelled in the freedom, expressing every passing thought in a series of wild aerobatics, sky-writing his emotions. Eventually, he became tired and let himself glide on outstretched wings, following a meandering, silvered river towards a small town.

He swept low amongst the chimney pots and TV aerials, aquiline eyes picking out the treacherous power lines. Earth-bound people crawled leadenly along the dusty streets and milled around the shabby shopping arcades. As he circled over a fuming roundabout his eyes were drawn to the open windows of a tall, crumbling house. He flapped his weary wings and flew towards the house.

As he reached the window, the man stretched his wings wide and pulled his head back to slow himself. He grasped the window-sill with his clattering claws and folded his wings. He rested, exhausted by his aerial exertions. After a while, he focussed on the room behind the window, a shadowy kitchen with a table in the centre. On a chair by the table, sat a naked man, his head thrown back. The handle of a knife and part of the dull metal blade protruded from his ribs, just below the heart. A dark liquid pool lapped at the wooden table-legs and trickled under the grimy fridge.

The silent room was reflected in the dead man's eyes: an empty glass on the table and at the window, a large bird that sat and stared. After some time, the bird turned and flew swiftly from the house.

Richard Kemp

Untitled

By

SHARON GILL

A just man stopped me,
He was wearing red and green
And seemed
To be a King
Powerful almighty.

He talked to me of right and wrong
And the path that lay between,
That of his queen,
Her joyous way a life of song.

A hawthorn tree then approached me
And told me he knew the way,
And had to say
It was well worth the trouble to learn to sing
And bring a little sunshine to the earth.

This is the path of justice
Between the black pillar and the white,
Through the doorway of the temple of the moon,
Come soon.....
and walk with us man and tree.

KGB

by

DAVID BROWNING

    He was clad entirely in black - a black leather trilby and a long black leather overcoat, the very epitome of a KGB agent. You wouldn't have been surprised if he had the letters embroidered in his hat band to complete the picture. He was addressing a small group of fellow Russians in a small Armenian bar, close to the Russian Embassy, in Tehran. His comrades were all listening respectfully, merely uttering the odd "Niet" or "Da" when there was a pause in the black leather diatribe.

    Bill Edmundson and I were regulars in that bar - it was run by an unsmiling Armenian who served vodka and beer with pickled cucumbers and bread to young Russians in regulation Eastern European suits. He always seemed ill at ease and gave the impression that tragedy had just struck his life or was about to do so. The bar was so close to the embassy that it was actually referred to locally as the "Russian Embassy".

    The Russians only had to cross Avenue Stalin to enter this refuge from the people's Soviet and they made the most of this little taste of freedom - even at ten o'clock in the morning when most people would drink a small vodka or perhaps a beer or two, the comrades would share a whole bottle of Vodka between three and mix it with just one Coca-Cola.

    Avenue Stalin had come into being after the Tehran Conference of 1943 when several main thoroughfares of the Iranian capital were renamed to commemorate that historic meeting of the wartime allied leaders. Avenue Roosevelt and Avenue Churchill also appeared and remained so until they were erased by the Ayatollahs following the revolution of 1979.

After Stalin's death he was publicly denounced by Khrushchev - who described to the world just how ruthless the Generalissimo had been and how dangerous it was even to look him in the eye. It explained why the standing ovations for Stalin's speeches used to go on and on ad nauseam - the first man to stop clapping was likely to wind up in the Siberian gulags. The new Russian leaders made repeated diplomatic efforts to obliterate Stalin's name from their neighbour's capital, but the Iranians were adamant in their refusal to change anything. Being in the western camp they enjoyed niggling the bear in this small way - so all through the cold war the address of the Russian Embassy was still Avenue Stalin, Tehran, even though the once all powerful tyrant had become a non-person - his embalmed body removed from the Lenin mausoleum in Red Square and spirited away at dead of night to be buried in an unmarked grave.

In the "embassy" the Russians were distinctly cold to outsiders, in fact in the space of more than two years not one had spoken to either Bill or I, the Russians always averted their eyes when there seemed any danger of contact - they seemed to fear capitalist contamination. On this particular day to our surprise, as Bill approached the bar, even before he had ordered, the man in black spoke directly to us. He asked who we worked for, what we did, where we worked, and what we thought of Iran and the Iranians. We were very noncommittal in our replies, for in those days you never knew when SAVAC, the Iranian Secret Police, might be listening and anyway we regarded it as very bad practice to criticise the host country, especially to the "enemy". As it happened the following week Bill was going up to Helsinki to marry his Finnish girlfriend and he was stopping over for a night in Moscow. He turned the tables on the KGB and became the questioner.

"Do you know Moscow very well ?" he asked.

"Very well, of course," came the reply.

"Well I'll be there next week and I'd like to see the sights, preferably off the tourist track," said Bill, and getting out his diary and pen he handed them to KGB, and asked him to note down unusual places of interest and sketch how to get there from Moscow airport.

The other Russians were very agitated and nervous at this fraternisation, and aghast at their minder making notes and sketch-maps in this capitalist's notebook. They seemed to press themselves hard against the wall and would have melted through and disappeared altogether if they had been able.

The next day I was walking along Avenue Stalin when who should I see coming towards me but that same black leather clad figure. I slowed my pace in preparation for the expected greeting and pleasantries intending to chat, but as soon as the man in black spotted me he quickly crossed to the other side of the road ignoring me completely, as though he had never seen me in his life before.

In the seventies when Mohammed Reza Pahlavi was Shah of Iran, the Russian Embassy itself was more fortress than diplomatic residence. Surrounded by a high wall above which projected the tops of ugly concrete apartment blocks, its single entrance had two separate steel gates - one for pedestrians, one for vehicles - both electrically operated from the gatehouse, manned 24 hours round the clock. Opposite these gates was a street of some older buildings with several more modern lock-up shops. Walking south, away from the embassy, you came upon the Russian School, surprisingly outside the embassy compound, in a little back street. The great wooden doors were usually open and you could glimpse an enormous portrait of Lenin in heroic stance and the red flag, with hammer and sickle, completely covering the far wall of the entrance hall. A few steps further on was Michaelian's, an Armenian pork butchers who sold cooked meats and sausages of all sorts - German bratwurst and beerwurst, salami, ham, bacon - all hidden by an L-shaped entrance way so that passing Moslems would not be offended. The counter assistants always gave you a taste of anything you were about to buy before you ordered - and they loved children. Children shopping with their parents would be offered so many tit bits that they never needed any tea after a visit to Michaelian's.

Further down on the other side was another vodka shop, smaller and rather less salubrious than the "embassy" - this was known as "Rosy Nose's" on account of the owner's truly wonderful appendage. As well as the usual alcoholic drinks he also served domboloms - sheep's sweetbreads that he sliced delicately on the bar in front of you, then dipped the slices in breadcrumbs and deep fried them in ghee. As an alternative you could have ghusht, cold beef cut in chunks - and with either of these delicacies French bread and pickles were included.

I was in "Rosy Nose's" one lunch time having a solitary beer, when a commotion started in the street outside. A small crowd had gathered around my car, a Peykan - the locally assembled Hillman Hunter Saloon - and when I looked out they shouted to me and pointed to the bonnet. A wisp of smoke was coming from the air vents. I immediately went about doing exactly the wrong thing. I opened the driver's door, leant in and disengaged the bonnet clip. I then scampered round to the front of the car and raised the bonnet, whereupon the entire engine compartment burst into flames. I was stunned and helpless but to my amazement a man in black pushed through the crowd producing a fire extinguisher and with a few well aimed strokes he put out the flames. I dropped the bonnet and turned to thank the black knight but the good deed had been performed and the leather clad figure had vanished. I was left surveying the smouldering, blistered bonnet of what had been my most prized possession - still nothing for it, I thought, and went back into "Rosie's" to finished my beer before hailing a yellow taxi to take me home.

The first car I owned in Tehran was an ancient Volkswagen Beetle with sliding roof - it was for ever getting its wings dented in the vastly congested streets of the capital, so I used to wait until all four were damaged and then have them all repaired at the same time, it was cheaper that way. Actually I hired this car to begin with from a Dutch-Chinese or Chinese-Dutch by the name of Ken Huang. He was an instrument engineer with the firm that had hired me, quite out of the blue, on the recommendation of a pseudo-Welshman who later came to hate my guts. Ken's heart was not really in engineering, trading was more his passion. His wife, a very prim and long suffering Dutch lady, said that she tried not to become too attached to possessions around the house because Ken would trade just about anything for anything else, if the opportunity ever arose. So after a month's hire period when the car had proved itself to be a very nice little runner and I had received my first salary in a comforting mix of Dutch guilders and Iranian rials, my feelings of insecurity became somewhat diluted and I bought the Beetle. To arrive at the sale price I had to bargain with the smiling Ken Huang, who really had me over a barrel as the local prices for second-hand cars bore no relation to the price levels that I was used to in UK. I can't remember what we finally agreed, but since the car gave me ten years comparatively trouble free motoring, I reckon I got a bargain.

It was about that time that Bill became what he described as the founder member of the "Crook Lock Club". His transport was a late model Peykan with twin carbs, leather upholstery and "go-faster" wheels. Although car theft was in its infancy, Bill decided to keep one step ahead of the local car recycling fraternity and invested in an early model Crook Lock - a device with a hook at each end and a lock in the middle. To immobilise the car you put one hook round the foot brake, the other round a spoke of the steering wheel, and turned the key in the lock.

One evening he was going to dinner at the commissary restaurant in the American Embassy, so he parked his car in the line of others outside, and feeling very pleased with himself for actually having remembered to set the Crook Lock, he went in to dinner. He met several friends in the restaurant and was invited to join them at a party afterwards. Never one to miss a booze-in he readily agreed and as a result found himself, many vodkas later, on Avenue Roosevelt in search of his car. The street was all but deserted with little traffic to get in the way - he jumped in, fumbled the key into the ignition and started off. At forty miles an hour he attempted a left turn.

"The Crook Lock, Oh! My God! The Crook Lock!"

In Tehran there are storm drains called "jubes" between the road and the pavement. These vary in width and depth. At this point they were 2ft wide and 2 1/2 ft deep. A complete left turn wasn't possible, the steering wheel wouldn't turn that far and he couldn't depress the foot brake. Bill went right across the boulevard, fortunately empty of traffic, both nearside wheels left the road, got trapped in the jube, and the car came to rest in a shower of sparks and rending metal. He was now the founder member of the "Crook Lock Club".

Since he was in vodka relaxed mode and his memory had extended to fastening his safety belt as well, he was dazed but unhurt. As he opened the door he felt himself gripped by the elbow and yanked onto the pavement. He was looking up at a familiar face beneath a black leather trilby.

"You OK ?", asked the man in black.

"Sure, sure", slurred Bill.

"You lucky to be alive !" said the man in black, and with that he turned and disappeared down a side street, leaving Bill to arrange for the recovery of the wreckage and to get home as best he could.

We never saw KGB again after that, maybe the rescue of a capitalist from a wrecked car was the last straw and his masters found him a nice little posting to the Steppes.

The Writers - Biographies

David Browning

David came to Devon in 1983 after an engineering career in the UK, the Middle East and Africa. He runs a stock farm and teaches Information Technology at East Devon College. He is married to Margaret who he met in Tehran, and has three daughters. He likes to write articles with a humorous or historical slant based on personal experiences.

Jill Cocker

Jill was born in Surrey and moved to Devon with her family when a teenager. She has a variety of career experience and now works in the human resources field. Her particular interests are horses and Devon country life. Her creative writing encompasses adult and children's stories and political debate.

Richard Gard

Living in a mill has provided insight into the influences affecting rural life. It is significant that Richard the Miller worked in the same building, centuries ago. The present Richard feels supported by his older namesake. A keen observer of life's little twists and turns and an insight into animal and human science provide a particular writing style. The pieces included cover the spectrum from light-hearted to serious.

Sharon Gill

Sharon is from Devon and writes poetry, on mainly mystical and magical themes, when her two year old son allows her the time.

Richard Kemp

Richard grew up in the Crediton area and studied at Q.E.C.C. His writing is full of surprises with a distinctive style that keeps the reader on their toes. He writes mainly short stories, often with a futuristic theme.

The Writers - Biographies

Jeff Kingaby
Jeff was born in Hertfordshire and on retiring from the police force moved to "West Aish", Morchard Bishop where he and his wife converted a derelict farmyard and currently run two self catering cottages. He recently edited the successful "Morchard Bishop Souvenir Programme" which recorded the village history during the war, and is one of a team researching a book "Morchard Bishop in the 20th Century".

June Lukins
June and her husband George moved from Herefordshire to Crediton in 1991, leaving behind their grown-up children. She is an enthusiastic Grandma of five, keeps sheep and cooks and gardens furiously, when in the mood. She is a keen motorcyclist touring as far and wide as commitments will allow. She writes poetry, short stories and articles ranging from human rights issues to motorcycling topics.

Rachel Maggs
Rachel grew up in Devon and returned with her husband and young daughter in 1994, after working in Somerset. She lives on a smallholding near Crockernwell and specialises in short stories.

Val Williams
After a busy life nursing and producing a large family who in turn produced an even larger number of grandchildren, she retired to a village near Crediton a few years ago. Time at last to explore the beautiful Devon countryside and watch the great variety of wild life at close quarters. Despite part-time work with the elderly she has taken the opportunity of a less frenetic life style by writing again, preferring short stories with a sting in the tail.

Printed on recycled paper by
HEDGEROW PRINT
The Old Creamery, Lapford, Devon EX17 6AE
Tel: 01363 83868 • Fax: 01363 83921